Dear Ahed....

The Game of War and a Path to Peace.

Written by Alberto Portugheis, Argentinean born concert pianist and Peace campaigner, *Dear Ahed* is a collection of radical and compassionate essays and letters demonstrating that through 'education', through understanding the way words are used, a society could be created that is free from war.

Alberto Portugheis explores how and why language has been used to separate societies, to control and antagonize people, demonstrating, how today, well educated and talented writers with extensive knowledge of the lexicon and assistance of psychologists together with scientists who have great expertise on mind control, help politicians organise chaos, violence and wars as they use techniques to create fear in the population, so that they can offer us protection.

'We should not underestimate the capacity of well-run propaganda systems to drive people to irrational, murderous, and suicidal behaviour'.

'We need not stride resolutely towards catastrophe merely because those are the marching orders'. **Noam Chomsky**

'The majority of politicians, on the evidence available to us, are interested not in truth but in power and in the maintenance of that power. To maintain that power it is essential that people remain in ignorance, that they live in ignorance of the truth, even the truth of their own lives. What surrounds us therefore is a vast tapestry of lies, upon which we feed'.
Harold Pinter (Nobel Prize Acceptance Speech).

'Dare to Know.'
Kant

Opus Publications
Incorporating
Opus Books & Opus Musica

Many of these letters have been posted on the Internet. First published in book form 2008.

ISBN: 978-0-9561536-0-9

© Alberto Portugheis

A democracy is nothing more than mob rule, where fifty-one percent of the people may take away the rights of the other forty-nine.

Thomas Jefferson

The People versus the Powerful is the oldest story in human history. At no point in history have the Powerful yielded so much control. At no point in history has the active informed involvement of the People, all of them, been more absolutely required.

William Rivers Pitt

If I know something that would serve my country but would harm mankind, I would never reveal it; for I am a citizen of Humanity first and by necessity, and a citizen of France second, and only by accident.

Montesquieu

Even if you are a minority of one, the truth is the truth.

Gandhi

Our only hope today lies in our ability to recapture the revolutionary spirit and go into a sometimes hostile world declaring eternal hostility to poverty, racism and militarism.

Martin Luther King, Jnr,

PHOTO: RONALD STEIN

ALBERTO PORTUGHEIS

*'My interest lies in educating people, in making them think and understand **why** we do not have a world at Peace. Together we can create a new economic system for the world that will not depend on the weapon business.'*

'Alberto is a man with a vision. He just loves all people regardless their race, religion or nationality. He is crying to all his friends or partners in many Peace Groups about the weapons industry and how effective their lobby is. Alberto is looking for justice, fairness and equality among all people in this world. Alberto deserve to be called a wonderful peaceful man'. AHED S. HUSSEIN.

Contents

Introduction	11
Foreword	21
1. No Matter Which Way I Turn	29
2. One God, One Country	38
3. Message of Christmas?	52
4. Lord Putnam and Bullying	61
5. Peace and Truth Seekers	69
6. Good Fences Make Good Neighbours	78
7. On Peace Memorials	85
8. On Power	97
9. War on Terror	111
10. Terrorists and Suicide Bombers	117
11 Full Spectrum Dominance	126
12. We Are All Born As People	134
13. Communism, Prejudice and Belief	142
14. The Un-jailed Bomber	157
15. Lines to a Poet	163
16. About Politicians	172
17. Human Rights	195
18. Hope	203
19. Paranoia, Truth and Journalism	215

20. Leftist Questions	223
21. Whose Child is this?	231
22. Politics and Religion	240
23. Children	253
24. Why War? Why Palestine?	265
25. Notes to a Palestinian Journalist	279
26. Bureaucracies, Fear and Strong Opinion	295
27. Education	305
28. Conversation with a Journalist	314
29. The Way I See Things	335
30. In the Beginning is the End	346
31. The Game	368
32. The Path for Peace	381
About the Author	404

Dedicated to Ahed Hussein and to all my friends who are seeking Peace and Truth, both those in the Peace and Dialogue Forum with whom I exchange ideas, and the millions that I do not know.

I also dedicate this book to my dear late father, Simon Portugheis.
He fuelled my disapproval of war and militarism and inspired my quest for world Peace.

INTRODUCTION

ALBERTO PORTUGHEIS is a Peace Worker, Peace Activist, Peace Campaigner, a person who is in regular contact with the people from many troubled areas of the world – Palestine, Israel, Nepal, Sri Lanka, Burma, Iraq, and several African and Latin American countries.

He received a nomination for the Nobel Peace Prize in 2008. Dejan Sinadinovic, describes him as a man of *'conviction,'* with a *'vision of a world with no armies and no war'* –a vision he described as *'revolutionary'* where *'relationships between people will be richer'* when *' it is no more based on fear and hatred'*.

Alfred Nobel's ideal was of ' *a demilitarised world order, with fraternity among nations'*. Alberto Portugheis shares this vision. On the web of the Nepal Conflict Study Centre, where he is a respected advisor, he says, 'No matter which way round I turn arguments, from which perspective I look at conflict - out of a thousand perspectives - there is no way I can see a solution to conflict, to war, to the present state of world affairs, whilst we continue to accept a militarised world'.

Alberto Portugheis has made careful analysis of the reasons behind war and conflict – the very fact that weapons are produced and governments procure them to maintain Peace is an absurdity: *'The list of weapon manufacturing countries is very long.'* He says, *'Even longer is the list of weapon buying countries, which are ready to go bankrupt for the sake of having arms.* **Having arms as a deterrent is as logical as providing musical instruments to deter people from playing and listening to music'**.

He is a man who works internationally, tirelessly, towards the demilitarised world that Nobel held as his ideal. Some of you may know of his ideas from his interventions at the European Network for Peace and Human Rights Conferences at the European Parliament in Brussels, or at Ministry for Peace meetings in the British Parliament. He says, *'I wish an end to war because of respect for human life, justice for humankind, happiness and well being for every human on this earth. We are all born with this right but **peace will NEVER be achieved whilst Governments continue to pay scientists to invent or develop weapons - even when thanks to weapon manufacturing, un-employment figures are kept under control. The Arms Trade provides Governments of weapon-producing countries, as well as agents – often diplomats or politicians of weapon-buying countries, with very considerable profits'**.*

That Portugheis promotes Nobel's ideal of *'brotherly love'* through his music and his vision for peace is clear. '***Above all***,' he says of war, '***the same hatred is caused in survivors, the same feelings of revenge towards the attackers. Unless we campaign against all weapon development, invention and manufacturing, there is no way a campaign against the weapon trade can be effective'***.

'If we did not arm countries' stresses Alberto Portugheis, *'they would not need Gandhi's example. Arming people and telling them to live in Peace is the same as giving a pound of chocolate or honey to someone every day and telling him not to gain weight. It is simply absurd.'* He emphasises that unless we *'understand that we must get rid of weapons first, cries for Peace, Justice and Human Rights will never be heard'*.

He knows *'a demilitarised world would initially mean mass unemployment,.'* saying that, *'Government treasuries and businesses alike would need a contingency plan to re-adjust to a world that 'only' functions well **without** wars.* Other employment for the mutual good of both humankind and the planet would soon take the place of military and war activities.

His interest is in **educating** people, in making them think and 'understand' why we have not yet managed to achieve a world at Peace in spite of a myriad of diplomatic interventions, Peace Treaties and 'peace keeping' operations by military powers. He calls on social and economic philosophers, on governments across the world, and on each one of us, urging, *'We must work **together** on how we can create a new economic system for a world that will not depend on the weapons business.'*

The messages of support for his nomination for the Nobel Peace Prize came from across the world, many from those who have suffered war first hand - from Israel, Argentina, England, Netherlands, Italy, Taiwan, France, Brazil, Germany, Spain, Austria, USA, Croatia, Norway, France, Serbia, Tasmania, Australia, Chile, Greece, Hungary, Belgium, Singapore, Mexico, Switzerland, Slovenia, Russia, Wales and Scotland.

People have clearly been touched by the message that Alberto Portugheis brings. *'Alberto is a man with a vision. He just loves all people regardless their race, religion or nationality. He is crying to all his friends or partners in many Peace Groups about weapons industries and how effective their lobby is. Alberto is looking for Justice, fairness and equality among all people in this world. He deserves to be called a wonderful peaceful man, and I hope he can win the Nobel Prize'*, wrote Palestinian, Ahed Hussein. The musician, Alfredo Corral, wrote from Argentina, *'Not one day goes by, without Alberto doing or saying something that shows his tenacity and worry. He accepts his self-imposed challenge of ridding the world from weapons, with great courage. His campaign for disarmament and for a more peaceful and just world deserves recognition on a worldwide stage'*.

Enrique Fernandez Romero, from Belgium (Euro Parliament) wrote, *'The world needs to hear Alberto Portugheis's message loudly and clearly,'* while Wissam Boustany, Founder of 'Towards Humanity' (Lebanon/ UK) urged him, *'Keep shouting at the top of your voice, Alberto. The arms trade and militarism in general must be exposed for what they truly are - they are contemptible and destructive for humanity. No wars are being fought in my name.'*

The writings and thoughts of Alberto Portugheis force us to reconsider the construction of societies and international relationships.

JOHN LEECH has worked in the European and Atlantic fields and has had a long association with the Commonwealth Development Corporation, with assignments in Africa, South-East Asia and the Indian subcontinent. He has published books on NATO and West European issues. He was Assistant Director of the NATO Parliamentarians' Conference and European Co-ordinator of the American-European Political and Security Circle West-West Agenda. He is a leading member of the Federal Trust.

Publications include:
Halt! Who Goes Where? The Future of NATO in the New Europe (1991), and *Asymmetries of Conflict: War without Death (2002)*

London. August 2008.

Dear Reader,

Before you read this book, I would like you to know that you are about to embark on a strange experience. Normally, Music is composed by musicians/composers, paintings are produced by painters and books are written by writers.

*What you have here is a book **not** written by a writer. Of course, like many other musicians, or politicians, for that matter, I could have asked a talented 'ghost' writer for help. However, I neither had the funds nor the attraction to doing it.*

I must therefore apologize, to all those with infinitely more knowledge and mastery of the English language - not my mother tongue - to forgive the construction of sentences, the repetition of words where attractive synonyms would, I am sure, have been used by a 'real' writer.

A second apology is due. More than an apology, really. I would say, a 'request for forgiveness', from politicians, diplomats and spies. My book may give you the impression that I refer to 'all of you'. However, I can assure you, this is not the case. I have known, politicians, diplomats and spies, who are excellent professionals and wonderful human beings. And there are, of course, thousands I have never met.

This apology includes scientists who invent weapons, employees in weapon factories and the military who kill and are killed. All of them have a family to feed and many of them do not have any other option in life than to follow murderous marching orders.

Probably the most important request for forgiveness, and at the same time as a plea for understanding, I make to religious people, or, even if not practicing a religion, believers in God, a Creator of the Universe.

I have, never in my life, been able to believe in such God. To be totally accurate, when I say 'never', I mean since I started to read and write, play the piano and meet with Life. By Life I mean human beings, animals, plants, - including the poisonous variety - flowers, mountains, lakes and seas, health and illness, happiness and un-happiness, justice and injustice, car, train and other vehicle accidents, natural catastrophes, earthquakes, lightning, floods, erupting volcanoes, torrential rains, draughts, war and peace.
To me, nothing, absolutely nothing of what happens to us, or happens to Earth, is the will of a God. I believe in Nature and in Evolution. To me, there are un-controlled Forces of Nature that determine changes in our environment, our planet, and then, there is the Universal, Mystic Law of Cause and Effect. Whether 'Nature'

produced or 'Man produced' what we live and experience is always the effect of a cause.

I believe 'Man' has been, is and will always be responsible for his own actions. This means that wars, which are infallibly always 'entirely' man produced, could be changed for peace.

This is my plea and pledge.
Alberto Portugheis

DEAR AHED…

Alberto Portugheis

With a Foreword by John Leech

FOREWORD

'PEACE,' wrote Milton, 'hath her victories no less renowned than war.' And also its foot soldiers, those who toil against seemingly insuperable odds of tradition, national pride and age-old mindsets, oblivious to hostility and worse. Classic martyrs in a high moral cause, often unknown in their homeland but revered among the people whose burdens they assume; such is Alberto Portugheis. The apparent absurdity of one man seeking to change a global system, to fell an empire of the super-rich and übermighty, invites comparison with Gandhi. There are few satisfactions in this endeavour, only the firmness of the stepping stone they succeed in hewing out of the unforgiving rock impeding man's ascent.

If mankind is to progress, we need visionaries ready to stake out a far-off future with far-out ideas. Ideas, however utopian, are idle only if the very first building block does not lie close at hand. In the banishment of war, the ground prepared since the end of World War II already offers substantial footholds from which to launch credible beginnings. Many structures are in place for crisis management, for conflict prevention, for international monitoring, for multilateral diplomacy, for an effective panoply of intervention mechanisms. Too painstaking, too prone to being overridden or subverted by power politics, they will not figure among the Author's chosen instruments. His message is clear: if no one profited from distributing arms to provoke such conflicts, there would be no need for the machinery to still them. But if we let our horizons be darkened by those assaults which daily occupy our screens, we will never become conscious of the many hundreds of conflicts averted and prevented from becoming news. As with our local media, what makes the news are those relatively few cases of savagery which need to be seen against the background of millions of us going peacefully about our business, without criminal intent or interference.

Even if the ground is ready, the task remains herculean. Our identity is born of a sense of belonging: to family, community and nation. All of these are currently eroding. Life within the family gets steadily shorter, the links within it more tenuous. The interests of the immediate community have been sacrificed to the workplace. And the certainties of nation and sovereignty are being superseded by larger political entities through which we need to assure and assert our values. That state of flux and the search for identity are exemplified by the debate about the European Union. Many find the answer in ignoring both. And yet the talismen continue to be laid in our cradle: attitudes to right and wrong, action and reaction, tales of distant wars, of heroes and national icons. A hazy trailer of 'what made us great', the date of some famous battle, an impression without anchor in a perceived historical process. No context of the human travail that demanded such sacrifice. The progression of human renewal means that each generation is born into the world devoid of a sense of history, of what brought them to their time.

If that presents a hazard, it also offers an opportunity. Our children are our reincarnation, born without memory and with fresh minds waiting to be excited. The accretions of the past, all the painful and tawdry baggage of our ancestors which fashioned their traditions and our legacy is not necessarily eternal. For brief moments, usually in late adolescence and early retirement, we find the free will to size up our situation and responsibilities. If reform is possible, it must start there.

What applies to individuals goes even more for the institutions they create. Here the Portugheis model faces perhaps its most daunting task, for these are even more difficult to reform than the hearts of warring men. Even Goethe, amongst his other accomplishments an able public administrator, thought that, 'It is impossible ever to defend or praise an institution,' because with time the great ideas on which they are founded invariably become tyrannical. So the main question to be asked of this book is, 'How can it be done?' It would be idle to demand a full blueprint; but legitimate to ask what should be the first step.

The answer lies in what should also be a warning to the reader. The book is written for the world, not a British, American or European audience. Hence its strictures do not apply in equal measure to all countries and the reader must beware of feeling aggrieved by seemingly false charges – but instead reflect on the appalling truth that they still apply to many others. Yet herein, too, lies hope. It is precisely the fact that several countries are already a longish way towards a realisation of what Portugheis' holy grail might look like in practice that makes it possible to discern the way forward. The literature supporting his endeavours is expanding, as is the academic interest. And a whole discipline has already evolved around the intensely practical and parallel field of nuclear non-proliferation, with its repeated – if so far ineffective – homage to full disarmament.

The whole book is, of course, a testament of love. It speaks of the wounds he suffers by taking all the world's anguish and misery into his enormously receptive heart. The map of the suffering created and 'contrived' by his giant adversaries is also the chart of his own calvary among the millions of afflicted people. The fact that he is an accomplished musician makes him the more open and sensitive to the fate in which they are caught up. The resonance within his own being is starkly reflected in his accounts. It is not necessary to agree with every word of his homilies to understand and be pierced by his chilling message.

Is there perhaps already a turn of the tide? Are the worms already gnawing at the military option from within? What the generals call 'overstretch' is the approach of limits to men willing to be recruited and the ability of treasuries to pay for their expeditions. Even without the compulsion of the arms race of the Cold War, is the 'Trillion Dollar War' now edging the West towards the same point at which the Soviet Union had to cede?

As I write this, I read that British troops are to scale back attacks on the Taliban after killing 7,000 insurgents in two years of conflict. Why not kill more? Because British commanders fear that the deaths are a boost to local recruitment 'as the dead insurgent's family feels a debt of honour to take up arms against British soldiers'. Generals, it seems, are quicker to realise the truth than those who send them to war. Even Napoleon had at last to confess, 'There are only two powers in the world: the sword and the mind. In the end the sword is always conquered by the mind.'

                                  John Leech   2008

Dear Ahed...............

1.
NO MATTER WHICH WAY ROUND I TURN

No matter which way round I turn arguments, from which perspective I look at conflict - out of a thousand different perspectives - there is no way I can see a solution to conflict, to war, to the present state of world affairs, whilst we continue to accept a militarised world.

A country does not need to be governed by a military dictatorship in order to qualify for the name of 'Military Nation'. Any country in the world that has Armed Forces 'IS' a 'Military Nation'.

Now, what is the point in having Armed Forces, spending fortunes in training thousands - millions in some countries – of people, paying their salaries, buying weapons, air-fighters, tanks, warships, uniforms, spying devices, torture instruments, and all of the other atrocities of war hardware?

Certainly NOT to then have soldiers, marines, pilots and their bosses, all sitting in their barracks or ships, playing cards, watching TV, enjoying a beer, playing computer games or going to the theatre.

What is the point in Governments spending so much in weapon research? Around 60% of Government funds allocated to Universities and Institutes of Higher Education are devoted to military aims. Over 40% only is allocated for everything else – for instance, education, transport, health, environment, and any other human need. In the US, over half a million scientists receive their salaries and their funds for research from the military budget of the Washington Administration. The list of weapon manufacturing countries is very long. Even longer is the list of weapon buying countries, which are ready to go Bankrupt for the sake of having Armed Forces.

Weapon manufacturing countries also use the war industry in order to keep unemployment figures down and boost the funds for their Treasury. For the US, weapon research and manufacturing not only has these advantages, it also helps the country work towards her aim of achieving Full Spectrum Dominance, as announced and encouraged by Dwight Eisenhower.

In order to have Armed Forces, we have to develop a criminal mentality in people first – unless a country has a compulsory military service. Governments use all their power in order to develop in young people a love of violence through films and games.

Young people in prisons are people who did not have the patience to wait to grow up. In many instances they became criminals before their maturity. In fact, many of them do have a second chance of sorts - Armies look for recruits among the young men in prisons.

The criminal mentality or love of violence is installed in the citizenship by educating people first of all in Patriotism and Religion, the two main forces that separate humans. History is taught in every country of the world on the basis 'we are great, our country is great' implying 'other people and countries are not the same'. We are taught that we must be ready to give our life for our country. Military men who won battles have more streets, squares, buildings, etc, named after them, than writers, artists, scientists, sportsmen, etc. The squares and public buildings of the world are littered with statues, busts, and portraits of militarists that have won battles. Children are taught to admire them, with the idea that they will also wish to become heroes for their country.

Religions always teach 'they' have the Truth, implying other religions do not have it; therefore people practicing other religions are wrong or inferior. History is so connected to religion and murder that authorities insist on teaching the Inquisition and the Holocaust, so as to remind the world of what Christians thought of Jews.

The Crusades teach Christians hatred of Muslims and vice-versa. In parts of Spain to this day, anniversaries of battles between Catholics and Muslims are remembered, with populations disguised half as Catholics, half as Muslims, each group dressed differently, but all wearing 'masks' so as to not to recognize each other. They then proceed to hit each other with dozens of different tools or gadgets, many ending up in hospital each year.

Censorship is always used on love (sex in most cases). Something sexually provocative or explicit can easily be considered pornography by censors and not suitable for children and young teenagers. However, young people are allowed to watch the most terrifying violence and weapon use.

Films and games are used to produce future lovers of violence, future criminals, and future militarists. No matter the nightmares a violent film can cause a young person, censorship will never deny it a showing. Computer games approved by Governments are those where the player who kills the most is the winner.

Of course, I would not comment on this type of education if Governments were made of people who came from another planet. However, reality is that Governments are made of people who have received the education I describe above, brain-washed by Religion, school, nationalistic history and TV education. Politicians want to 'serve their country' and for them, this means, above all, making sure the country can defend itself.

Now, a country can defend itself only if it is attacked, so Ministers of Defence 'need' enemies, otherwise they cannot do their job properly.

The idea is that, if a country is very well armed, other countries will think twice before attacking. In other words, that good Armed Forces act as 'deterrent'. This would be acceptable in theory, but in practice the idea is impossible to accept. Weapons cost a lot of money and that money has to be found somewhere. This leads to endless corruption and re-routing of funds that should and could have been used for better and nobler aims, but more to the point, it leads to the necessity to create armed conflicts, even in perfectly clean deals and the absence of all corruption.

Arms as a deterrent are as logical as providing musical instruments and CDs, to 'deter' people from playing or listening to music. Having military schools and say you are working for Peace is as logical as having music schools with the aim of promoting silence.

Weapon manufacturers are not charitable organizations, which have nothing to do with their fortune and decided to make and give away their produce. They are commercial corporations who need to sell, not only to be able to pay their researchers, technicians and all type of employees, but also to have their produce tested and to make money for themselves.

Tests serve two important purposes: 1) For the manufacturer to see how his product works in order, if necessary, to improve it, and 2) as a 'show-case' to demonstrate that the product is good and thus gain further contracts.

In other words, in this world-view, armed conflicts should be promoted, MUST BE promoted, otherwise the industry collapses.

Most of us know that with only 8% of the money spent yearly on weapons, we could feed the world, put an end to homelessness, create jobs for everybody, develop the un-inhabited regions of the planet, end illiteracy and the killer diseases worldwide - plus a myriad more badly needed changes.

However, this would bring a balance to the world that the powers do not want. The powers want the Third World to remain Third World. This can only be achieved by promoting endless revolutions, conflicts big and small, installing - and removing – dictators, corrupting politicians and militaries, creating social unrest, injustice, hunger, civil wars, dependency. Diplomatic corps – very often without their knowledge - and secret services are used to this aim - all with the co-operation of the 'Illuminati', the Bankers of the world, who are the REAL rulers. The old maxim that 'Money makes the world go round' is horribly accurate. Trans-nationalism or Globalisation, including the arms industry, rules.

Dear Ahed,

A young man I knew got a job with a Muslim company because he holds a South American Passport. I say 'Muslim' and not Arabic, as I call EL AL a 'Jewish' company. No way they'd have employed him with an Israeli passport. And believe me, no matter how good he is at his job, he will never be offered a top position. And I can assure you, there are Muslims working in EL AL, like in many Jewish offices, hospitals, Banks and Schools. Again, they'll find promotions never come.

My friend, I know you read and know a lot about Islam and other religions. This is why I am sure you know I am saying the truth. I am not interested in 'interpretations', in what I or anybody else believes; I am only interested in THE TRUTH, in facts. My interest lies in educating people, in making them think. You say that, 'Religious individuals are wrong - but not religion itself'. You are, I'm sorry to say, very, very wrong. Religious people can be like you, good people, genuine peace lovers, respectful of human life, but it is Religion that dictates we cannot live in Peace and harmony.

Hope you're enjoying the festive season and also I send you my very best wishes for a healthy, happy and fulfilling 2008,

Alberto

2
ONE GOD ONE COUNTRY

There is no 'your God and my God'. For all people of monotheistic religions, God is ONE and the same.

I do not hate religions. I hate what people do with them. More, I hate the abuse of Human Rights. To me, imposed religions are the first abuses of Human Rights. Jews are taught that the Messiah has not yet come.

If this is what they believe, it means that they think that **all Christians** are wrong, that they worship an imaginary being. Jews can learn to respect Christians, but in their hearts, they are separate. By the same token, Christians are indoctrinated into rejecting Jews because of the refusal to accept Jesus Christ as the Messiah.

Some thinkers preach, correctly, for non-religious States, where everybody can practice the religion of its choice, all with the same civilian rights. There are many millions of people respecting other people's religion. Yet religious wars will continue because this is what organised religion is ultimately about. Why do you think that the Church and the Armed Forces are so linked? Why was Peron overthrown from a Government by military force? Because he opposed the Church. What was the Bishop of Paraguay doing in a Government cabinet meeting to decide the fate of their Vice President? Why is the Commission that chooses the Archbishop of Canterbury made up mainly of Politicians?

It is hard not to confuse the spiritual side of religion with the reality of their brutal control of people, with their association with Banks and the weapon business. It does not help the cause of Human Rights.

I tell Muslims and Jews, you started as brothers, half-brothers, cousins, you are all related. Both Jews and Muslims do not eat pork, both practice circumcision. Jews and Muslims are in reality like two brothers, only with some different tastes and life style. Brothers would not need to live in separate houses for these reasons. Even extremely happy couples can have different interests in life. The wife likes the cinema, the husband does not, the wife likes cakes, the husband likes meat and fish, the wife drinks tea, the husband coffee and so on.

What does it matter? If there is love and respect between them, there is no problem.

Look at the physical characteristics of Muslims and Jews. It is so easy to take a Muslim for a Jew and vice-versa. When Golda Meir and one of her Ministers went to a secret meeting with the King of Jordan, they dressed as Arabs and nobody noticed they were two Jews. In London I knew a family now living in South Africa, she an English Jewess, he a Muslim from Lebanon. Not only they looked alike, they were often taken for brother and sister.

Wars exist, as General Smedley Butler (1888-1940) said, 'for the suffering of the many and the benefit of the few'. 99.9 % of the world population does not want wars, but, for that elite tiny minority who runs the world, Peace is not good for business.

The best way they can have wars is by using religions to separate and antagonize populations, educating - brainwashing - people into thinking 'us and them'. And, if there were only one religion around, the powers would separate us by creating a 'left' and a 'right'. Monarchists or anti-monarchists, patriots. Anything that divides populations nationally or internationally is good business for the powerful.

Educating - brainwashing – populations into becoming violent, with a desire to kill, is part of the strategy used. Only by creating a group of people in each country, attracted to weapons and to killing, can you have armies. To choose as a profession becoming a General in the Army, commanding hundreds of soldiers to torture and kill innocent people, you really must have a deranged mind and heart.

The interesting thing is that these 'Generals' are human beings like you and me. They also like music, the cinema, football, food, having a family, living an ordinary life. When you see them all happy, playing 'father' with their children, you'd think ' that is the nicest man in the world'. However, deep down, they are longing for that moment when they can pull a trigger, throw a bomb, torture someone. Indira Gandhi used to call the military, 'the most irrational people on earth'. As I say, I do not blame them. They have been educated to be irrational. They do not even know what they are.

Marx wrote, 'Religion is the sigh of the oppressed creature, the heart of a heartless world, and the soul of soulless conditions. It is the *opium* of the people'. Theistic religions are also the poison of society. Divisive definitions like, 'your' religion, 'my' religion, 'their' religion, as well as ethnic or national brainwashing, are shared by all those in power. It is so easy to understand why we do not have Peace. Division stirred by concentration on feelings and thoughts of difference makes politicians and their Masters, the weapon industry, very happy indeed.

The hatred that can be aroused in our minds and the aggressiveness it can create in our words, are exactly the same as the hatred in the minds of politicians and the aggressiveness of their actions.

And what of the non-believers? Being an atheist does not mean you do not believe in spirits, or that you are a non-spiritual person. As a musician, I have to spend my life 'communicating' with the spirit of the composer, trying to understand what the composer wants to say, so that I can better transmit his/her message.

Leaving music and all other arts aside, my speaking about morality, kindness, generosity, compassion, justice, honesty, respect for human life, education, is ALL connected to the spirit, to the spiritual life of the individual, to spiritual values.

However, religions are exactly the opposite. They are all materialism. It is all about power. Every month, the Muslim hierarchy tells the world the number of Christians who converted to Islam and equally, the Christian hierarchy reveals the number of Muslim converts to Christianity, particularly Catholicism. The more famous the convert, the more the Press coverage.

It is said of Islam that it is more than a religion, that it is a complete way of life. The same is said about Judaism. Sometimes, Christianity is excluded from this group, saying that Christianity is more of a spiritual system of belief. Thanks to the astute words, 'Give what is God's to God', the Catholics have become the biggest religious empire in the world. Not only were they able to invade and conquer many countries, but also they have built an infinite number of palaces for themselves. Not only have they taken - and continue to take - millions from the rich, they even take from the poor and starving. With the clever ruse that the innocent, naive faithful are 'giving to God', bishops and cardinals can live in great luxury, travel the world 1st class, or like the Pope, have his own aircraft.

If Church and State were **really** separate, we would not have the Head of the Church of England, the Archbishop of Canterbury, chosen by a Church Commission that meets in Parliament and is formed by, mainly, politicians.

It has been put to me that in Islam there is no separation between religion and politics, that Caesar has nothing, since everything belongs to God. This is a **big** contradiction! If there were no separation, then everything would belong to everybody. In reality, nothing belongs to God and everything belongs to Caesar; that is to man or men.

God does not need money, does not need armies, and does not need torture, killings, invasions, wars, and power. All of this is wanted, not by God, but by 'man'.

I have also been asked if spiritual religion means that we should coexist with and adapt to idolatry. It is a nonsensical question. I never wrote anything that could imply this. If it is the understanding and definition of spirituality that one should worship the only God, the creator of the Universe, I do not share but respect this view.

I am a Buddhist. I try to separate fiction devised to control societies from 'facts'. Teaching fear of God is the best way in the battle to control people. The inaccuracies in the biblical stories do not bother me. If the death toll of a specific battle reported in the Bible is not quite accurate, it is neither here nor there. If instead of a reported killing of 10,000, the real figure might have been 6,000 or 20,000, what does it matter? If after invading a town we read Jews consumed the olive oil instead of almonds found in the newly occupied land, so what? What does it matter if, having experienced flood, exactly as it happens today, the Bible reports the flooding as worldwide? What does it reflect? Just that to the writers and historians of the day, the world equalled what they knew. They had no idea the earth was round, let alone how large it is.

It is not that I oppose religion 'per se'. To me, all religions are true. But the wars they cause are also horribly true.

Wars are the product of religions that teach of an Almighty

God, who has been sitting in the sky for billions of years and who decides our destiny.

Someone said to me, 'It is far easier to indulge the lust for revenge than it is to work towards non-violence.' Why? Because lust for revenge is taught to us, at school, through reading the Bible, through learning history. We are taught to love and admire those who won battles, never those who opposed them. We are taught, taught, taught and taught violence. This is why I insist that it is all a matter of Education.

Germans were not born with a hatred of the Jews. Hitler made them hate because it was needed for his political plans. Had Hitler taught his citizens to love Jews, the Holocaust could have never occurred. It does not take long to brainwash an entire population, as Hitler himself often said.

I do not use the Bible as a theistic book, as I do not believe in a supreme and eternal God. As I have already said, I am a Buddhist. I refer to the Bible as a history book. The battles that were fought, the invasions and atrocities committed, were just that, atrocities. They were all the decision of men, who used God as an excuse. This is still in practice today.

Not campaigning against militarism means not working for Peace. To argue about who should or should not live in Israel/Palestine is pointless while armies are created in the disagreeing groups. With our discussions we are only creating more reasons for Governments to encourage weapon research, development, manufacturing, trading and, of course, the use of weapons.

Look at the pictures from Iraq. The world is surprised, but I am surprised by the world. Nobody seems to realise that 'killing' is a pleasure for a professional military. Torturing, humiliating, degrading is far more interesting and entertaining.

The same applies if you are the pilot of a sophisticated air-fighter. You do not think at all about the hundreds you kill; you are only interested in, excited by, the fact that it feels so good, flying at high speed, proving your skills at reaching your targets with pin-point accuracy, obeying orders. Life has no value for the Military. This is why they go to military schools to learn how to extinguish it. The military have been dehumanised.

Think of the problems that created havoc in Ireland for centuries. The Majority are not interested in politics anyway and the general public does not like, does not want wars. For the Pope and his 'Cabinet', it is a very different story. The Vatican with its own Army fought many wars until its reputation was so tarnished it signed pacts with monarchs and all sort of rulers to fight on its behalf. There are plenty of documents from popes or other important clergymen in Rome, to Kings and Queens, reminding them there are the 'Arms of Rome'.

Many battles in Britain, Germany, France, Holland, between Catholics and Protestants, were fought 'on behalf' of the Church in the name of the one God. Also on behalf of the Church, various Monarchs and later on, politicians were assassinated. Even Popes, Cardinals and Bishops were murdered, if their ideas were felt to work against Rome's interests. Wars are decided by those at the top. They are frequently pursued against 'other religions' to gain power. In England for example, people have been misled to think the Queen does not interfere in politics. The reality is different. The only person who has the right to decide on war/s is the Queen. Prime Minister Blair could have never invaded Iraq without the Queen's approval.

My friends, PLEASE, try, at least TRY to understand what I am saying. Believe me, it is not my imagination running riot. I remember very well my conversations with young men who dreamed of a career - and glory - in the military. I remember what made them tick, the books with violent subjects that they read, the films they enjoyed watching, all reinforced by the 'education' they had received. Of course there were exceptions, but by and large, the military became to me synonymous with war, violence and injustice.

War means suffering, hunger and poverty for the majority, often done in the name of God. **Our** God versus **Their** God.

I repeat that for people of theistic religions, God is ONE and the same. Yet, they continue to place 'our' god against 'their' god and even make God a nationalistic Being. By calling members of the other religions 'infidels' the path to war is easily created. Furthermore, so strong is the power each religious group attributes to their 'God', they kill each other without hesitation. Muslim groups versus other Muslim groups. Christian groups versus other Christian groups.

Dear Ahed,

You wrote 'The bombing was carried out neither by Hamas nor by the Islamic Jihad. It was carried out by Fatah.' Does it really matter WHO did it? You have another group of innocent victims dead, including the bomber himself. What has that gained for the cause?

The bombing? All it does is to send the Army chiefs running for more weapons and to develop other ways of controlling Palestinians. It is dreadful.

As I have said to Khalid, unless he does not condemn this type of action in his writings, continuously and relentlessly, he is a not helping the cause of Peace.

You then say, 'Why did they do it? It is because they have lost hope in this world's ability or willingness to give them justice' You know very well that only words, from your pen, our pens, can generate justice by defying the lie of militarism.

You know very well that violence ONLY generates violence, that there will be more injustice, and more abuse of Human Rights.

I have written to tell Khalid that Palestinians have millions of supporters of justice, worldwide, from all religious groups. It is these supporters who are losing hope. I have said to him, 'Please ACT!!!!' in the hope that he will have the courage to go on and on and on telling the story of the way to peace via demilitarisation.

Alberto P.

3.

THE MESSAGE OF CHRISTMAS?

Having listened with great care to the Pope's 2007 Christmas message, I was greatly saddened. He is recognised as a learned man, some say a Holy Man. In our troubled times, I wanted to hear what he would say to the world.

A Catholic priest, Gustavo De Bonis, from Argentina, sent a message of support for my nomination for the Nobel Peace Prize. He wrote, '*As a Catholic priest and a pianist too, I support completely a human-kind without war, as is undertaken by you. God bless this idea*'. I had hoped the message from the Pope to the people of the world might have held this vision.

In Italy, a non-believing priest I know, said to me, 'Alberto, if you were a very close friend of the Pope (of any Pope) you would know that not even he believes in the Scriptures'. 'Religion is a battle for power, a business. Religion is Politics, Religion is Wars'. As I listened to the Pope's Christmas message in incredulity, I saw also the social division. It is years since the Church stopped singing the unacceptable verse in its ever-popular old hymn, 'All things Bright and Beautiful' with its image of

> *The rich man in his castle,*
> *The poor man at this gate,*
> *God made them high or lowly,*
> *He ordered their estate.*

The verse has long been abandoned in the name of so called 'Political Correctness', yet the division between that particular rich man in his castle and the poor man at his gate listening to his words, has never been more apparent. Listening and watching, the stark discrepancies of the Pope's wealth and extreme poverty of some of the people he was addressing, made my blood boil so much that I must comment in some detail on what I heard.

The Pope said: '*Man is so preoccupied with himself,*' humbly, I would like to suppose, including himself within this preoccupation. He continued, '*he has such urgent need of all the space and all the time for his own things*'.

While this may be true of some humans, it is difficult not to relate it to the Pope also, living in one of the biggest palaces in the world, using all that space himself and dedicating so much time to himself, *'that nothing remains for others'*. Perhaps this is why the Catholic Church is so rich, so very rich. It certainly receives but seldom gives away!

'For his neighbour, for the poor, for God.' Sadly, history shows this is an exact description of the Vatican, dedicated to its own business and to expanding and increasing its power and control.

'And the richer men become, the more they fill up all the space by themselves. And the less room there is for others.' Is this why the Vatican excludes so many? Adds even more disadvantage to so many?

'The spirit of Christmas', the Pope emphasised, *'should make everyone recognise the darkness of a world where many people were closed into themselves because they did not want to receive God or his message'.*

I listened to the professional, studied language and the Public Relations expertise! The *'darkness'* of which he spoke has been **brought about** by religion. But as a protagonist for the Catholic branch of the Christian Church, he wants people to believe that Jesus and Jesus alone 'IS the light'. This approach cannot solve the *'darkness' of the world'*.

'Do we have time for our neighbour who is in need of a word from us, from me, or in need of my affection? For the sufferer who is in need of help? For the fugitive or the refugee who is seeking asylum?' the Pope asked his audience.

Again, He humbly included himself in this *'we'*. But he is assuming that each one of us has no time for our neighbour. Is he, perhaps, recognising that he, too, has no time for his neighbour or for a sufferer in need of help?

'Do we have time and space for God? Can he enter into our lives? Does he find room in us, or have we occupied all the available space in our thoughts, our actions, our lives for ourselves?' the Pope questions.

A sceptical person must ask, is this a genuine or a false man? This leader of the Catholic Church must know very well that there are millions of people in the world who do not worship Jesus, or are atheists, but have time and space for their neighbours and sufferers in need of help. Yet he wants us to accept his personal world-view that a person is only good if he lets Jesus into his life. How different this is to the doctrine of the Dalai Lama, who has written[1] *'Love for others and respect for their rights and dignity, no matter who or what they are - whether we believe in God or Buddha, or follow some other religion or none at all, as long as we have compassion for others.'*

The Pope lamented, *'that the holiday has been dominated by materialism.'* But he gave his speech dressed with gold and diamonds from top to bottom. I can tell you, from my priest friends connected with the Vatican, that day the Pope had the most expensive meal with the most expensive wines before his speech – and he will do the same today as he does every day of the year. It could be agued that his own life is dominated by materialism.

Later, the Pope lit a peace candle and placed it at the window of his apartment.

With this simple gesture, the masses that he knows so little about and treats with apparent disdain, go home thinking 'What a good man. He wants peace!'

---

[1] Ancient Wisdom Modern World

When you know and understand the history in the struggle for power of the Vatican, a history of intrigue and murder, of business and wealth acquisition, you will understand that the last thing the Pope has on his mind is Peace.

Dear Ahed,

You are a real romantic soul, a poet, a philosopher. You write to me, 'Is there any event or something in your Buddhist religion you guys celebrate such as Eid, Christmas, Hanukkah some religious festival, so you can tell me Happy something or other?'

Ahed, people are torturing and killing each other BECAUSE of Eid, Christmas and Hanukkah and you find it a reason for celebrating and be merry and happy?

I cry.

Ahed, to me all these supposedly happy occasions or anniversaries are reminders of the tragedies caused by the same theistic religions. Look at any moment in history.

In Ireland, Catholic and Protestant Christians have been killing each other for over 400 years. The whole of Europe has been the stage for war after war, assassinated politicians and monarchs, all between Christian factions. In the Spanish Civil War, Catholics killed Catholics.

You seem to forget, or prefer to ignore, that all theistic religions, Judaism, Christianity and Islam, began as versions that we would call today 'political movements'. Movements that dedicated themselves to the acquisition of lands, expansionism, power and riches. The politics and culture of the period necessitated the creation of credible belief-systems. In fact, if you look deeply into the beginnings of Islam, you'll clearly see how its Prophet appears as a visionary political leader. It is also politics that encourages the formidable Islamic armies to invade and conquer so many lands. In the Arabic world, their success is seen as a sign that Allah is on their side, so people decide to adopt Islam.

Similarly, when Muslim armies enter India via Afghanistan and the Indus, mass conversions begin to take place. Disaffection with the local religions and the simplicity of Islam must have played an equal part in this process. Mohammed's combination of a monotheistic universalism and the equality of all believers before God was an active formula to those burdened with caste systems and religious hierarchies.

Now, from the moment Mohammed died and the enmity and violence between his widows and his descendants, both blood and political, to the present day, the Islamic world has been riddled with fights, wars, assassinations and so on. Ahed, you know the history of your religion.

Alberto.

4

LORD PUTMAN AND BULLYING

Lord Putnam's speech to the Anti-Bullying Alliance in April 2005 stays in my mind; not only because I agree 100% with what he said, but also because it was time that these things were said. The only detail that worries me is the fact that Lord Putman limited his comments on social violence to films. This, I feel, is true but not the complete or 'real' truth.

We live in a militarised world, even those of us who live in supposedly 'democratic' countries. It is especially these democratic countries, which have, one after another, changed compulsory military service for the Armed Forces as a career or profession.

To join the Army, Navy or Air Force of your own volition, you have to become a lover of weapons, you have to become someone with a desire to kill – and, of course, you have to be prepared to be killed. You have to be prepared to drop bombs onto various targets from a great height - bombs that will kill and maim untold numbers of people. You must also be prepared to send these lethal gadgets from land, sea or air. Military pilots, trained and high on the adrenaline of action, agree that active service is a great thrill, the most exciting part of their professional lives.

Warfare needs scientists, intelligent and educated individuals, prepared to spend their lives not in finding cure for medical problems, but in creating bigger and smarter bombs, that will kill more people and faster. Warfare also needs people who are prepared to torture political prisoners, prepared to make the suffering last as long as possible.

Of course, our educators and the military have first convinced young people that, even if they die young, it is a way to become a hero, famous, a part of the history of their country, of the world.

This is why, no matter how many Oscars they win, statues of film-makers or actors, will not adorn the public squares or Government buildings. But commanders, colonels, captains, Lieutenants, those who killed the most in battle, yes, they will have that honour.

Nobody seems to bother about this situation, because by the time people recognise these 'heroes', each one of us has already been 'educated' - brainwashed - into believing that we owe our lives to them. Thus, we admire and love them.

We start by being taught 'patriotism', to try to create in us a desire to one day emulate these heroes, to also become rich and powerful - and, if we become fabulous shooters, killers, avengers, we also have a chance to be made heroes of our country.

From an economic point of view, we have successive Governments, of any political colour, who must increase the funds coming into the Treasury. Our economists cannot think of any better way than through the arms trade, from miniature bullets and spying devises to gigantic warships and nuclear submarines and everything in between, guns, rifles, grenades, landmines, torture instruments, mortars, land, sea and air bombs and missiles, tanks, war-helicopters, air-fighters, military jeeps and military uniforms.

Manufacturers of the above products need to pay their staff and finance everything else connected with their business. Thus, the need to promote wars. Governments have no option but to support them, by helping them export their produce. This is how we manage to produce, to create wars in so many corners of the world.

Toys and 'Virtual' games are designed, with Government approval, and help produce weapon and violence-loving children, so that we can count on an Army for tomorrow.

Children play with DVD games where old people cross the street and instead of trying to save lives, to win the game you have to be the player who killed the most.

Governments of weapon-producing countries, all of them, in order not to upset weapon manufacturers and also not to increase un-employment, are willing conspirators of the war industry.

This and much more I would have liked to discuss with Lord Putnam in his campaign against bullying. I would have liked to demonstrate to him the nature of our bullying and war orientated society. How can we ask our children to fight the wars of the politicians, torture prisoners as well as a whole range of hostilities against the weaker members of their own age group without teaching them bullying in the first place?

Dear Ahed,

You have written to me explaining that since you decided to move to the United States you have noticed how unfair the treatments of the Muslims is. You tell me that you have become very sensitive towards any criticism or even jokes about Islam or Muslims, telling me that you were never like that before.

'Yes I am a Muslim man', you say, 'and I am proud to say that'. You tell me that you are not a good committed Muslim because you disagree on many issues with your Muslim friends. You tell me that you are not my enemy. You tell me this because you have not realised that I stand with you.

I am particularly saddened by this, Ahed, as you are one of the most enlightened and sensitive persons in this Forum. Through these lines, I'd like to remind you and all the other educated persons that I have very little time for writing, but I want to do it. I asked you before, please, do not take my generalisations, as a comment on you personally or on any particular group.

When I say Muslims, Jews or Christians do this or that, I refer to particular individuals, not to ALL Muslims, Jews or Christians.

Try to remember that I write as an atheist.

I did not say, 'Young Muslims can be rapists in London' as if this was a particular characteristic of Muslim young men!! Rapists can be of any religious background. I mentioned Muslims, because we were talking about the education given by the different religions.

You say Ahed, 'We do have great reputation as Muslims in the world to carry or hold very low percentage of all crimes generally.' Allow me to say, Ahed, Jews also have the same reputation for low percentage participation in crimes, generally.

My impression Ahed, is, that you forget, if the Muslim population is 5% of the total and 5% of crimes are committed by Muslims, it shows that people, regardless to which religion they belong, can become criminals.

If 96% of criminals in Italy are Catholics, it does not mean that Catholics are 'more' criminal. It only reflects the fact that Italy is inhabited mainly by Catholics. By the same token, prisons in Iran or Qatar are full of Muslim criminals. It is only natural, because the majority of the population are Muslims.

Prostitutes have no specific nationality or religion. Sometimes, they are forced to do their job; sometimes they work of their own volition and sometimes, for sheer necessity. Clients do not choose the prostitute because of their nationality or religion. They choose them according to their preferences: black, white, oriental, thin, fat, small, tall, young, middle age, good listeners.

You say, 'We do not punish our daughters for having sex with Christians or Jews only.' But to me, what is wrong is not the religion of the man, but the 'punishment'. Why punish your daughter? It is 'her' life. She should be free to live her life the way she chooses. If, for having sex before marriage, she then finds it difficult to get married and have a family, that will be her 'punishment'.

Of course, she could choose, like many Muslim girls, to go and live in a society where non-virgins have equal chances of getting married and the problem is solved.

Similarly, you say, 'I do not think you can call me ignorant for choosing this style of living voluntarily'. Then, you should respect your children and grandchildren, to also choose their individual style of life 'voluntarily'.

You say 'I admire these rules and I do believe I am respecting myself, my daughter and my society for keeping our health and mental life clean and clear'. And I say, 'You are a very lucky man, my friend'. I wish all people could say the same.

Alberto

5

PEACE AND TRUTH SEEKERS

Many writing in the 'Peace and Dialogue Forum' seem to be un-willing or incapable to see how Banks, weapon manufacturers, Press barons, Churches and of course politicians, are delighted at your disagreements and fury. This is exactly what they need in order to continue making money, develop their business and keep societies under their control.

You accuse each other the way Israeli Jews accuse Palestinians and vice-versa. Meanwhile, the Vatican celebrates. They do not need another Crusade, Inquisition or Holocaust. They very strategically arranged for Jews and Muslims to kill each other.

You do not realize that people at the top are all part of the same elite, no matter what country they belong to. Arafat became a very rich man by co-operating with the West in not allowing the Israeli/Palestinian conflict to end. The same of course, on the Israeli side of the operation.

None of you seem to consider how everything is planned, to the last Molotov cocktail mentioned in one of the messages. We read that Palestinians throw Molotov cocktails, but nobody writes about 'who' teaches them to make Molotov cocktails and who encourages them to throw these at Israeli soldiers.

You do not seem to be interested in the new materials developed at MIT in Boston, USA and other such military 'partners' or 'rivals', that must be tested against Molotov cocktails, other missiles and in desert temperatures. Nobody seems interested in new weapons that must be tested. We read about the education Israelis receive (that Palestinians are inferior people), but nobody seems to realize that this has nothing to do with Israel or Jews. A militarised world demands this education.

Do you think the American Armed Forces could have destroyed Iraq (and the Iraqi population) the way they did, if beforehand they had been lectured on what wonderful people the Iraqis are? Of course to get one man to kill another man just because of his Government or religion asks him, you need to brainwash him first.

Lastly, my 'leit-motiv': the Business. If you want Peace, Justice, Human Rights and the happiness of Humanity, you must first create new strategies for politicians. A country can go Bankrupt because of maintaining its armed forces even without a war, but individually, the politician involved in arms negotiations makes a fortune. This is all that matters to such politicians and diplomats who play the role of arms dealers.

You will have to understand that it is not manufacturers of bicycles or shoes, growers of fruit and vegetables, publishers of books, artists, etc, who donate BIG sums of money to Political parties. These come from the weapon manufacturers, big banks and oil barons. The only way politicians can re-pay the favour is by creating wars, no matter where. But they'll always say to the electorate they are working for Peace. A real oxymoron to make Peace with War. It is as if a doctor said to his patient, 'To make you healthy, I must first give you an ulcer or a tumour'.

Look at the recently retired (forcibly removed) British Prime Minister, Tony Blair. He will be working towards creating more weapon business and wars in the world, particularly in the Middle East. For this he has been appointed by a quartet:

US, Russia, The European Union and the United Nations. However to confuse the public, they gave him the title of 'Peace' Envoy.

Another former British Prime Minister, John Major, after leaving Government, became the European representative of Carlyle, the biggest US weapon conglomerate, whose main shareholders are the Bush and Bin Laden families.

Look at Mark Thatcher, the son of another former British Prime Minister, Margaret Thatcher. He was introduced, by his mother, to the Saudi Royal Family and to the 'family' business, weapons. Today he is a multi-millionaire.

Former US President Clinton has also 'introduced' many people to the weapons (and drug) business. Reagan made a colossal fortune from the weapons business. Listen to President Bush today, defending the US strategy in Iraq. Of course, he has done what was right to keep all the weapon industrialists who donate to the party, happy, very happy. To Bush, how many US soldiers or civilians die, is neither here nor there. His duty is to help the war industry and in the process, help his own family business, oil.

As I write violence is spreading across Tibet and neighbouring regions, and the Chinese regime is right now making a crucial choice between tougher crackdown and dialogue. However, it is not that 'the Tibetans are sending out a global cry for change' that is the reason for this situation. It is the 'means' used by CIA - on behalf of the USA Government, Banks, weapon manufacturers and other interested parties.

Violence 'has' to spread. Apart from the obvious political/ideological reasons, there is the 'Business'. As in other countries, Chinese riot Police 'must' be used. Riot gear, uniforms, protection screens, tear-gas bombs, the paraphernalia of war, 'must' be used, consumed or damaged. We pay commissions to the Chinese - as we do with people around the world - for them to spend more on their riot Police and armies.

The CIA trains people on 'how' to revolt, how to organise revolts. Dialogue exists all the time. During this particular 'dialogue', it was decided that a violent crackdown would be performed. Exactly the same as happens with all conflicts. The Falklands war was pre-negotiated; the invasion of Iraq was pre-negotiated. Dialogue exists all the time. This is why diplomats are in place. Sometimes they do the 'job' of creating violence by themselves; sometimes they require the assistance of secret agencies.

The US Ambassador in Iraq only left Iraq after his mission of organising the invasion of American and British troops was accomplished. To achieve his mission, he dialogued daily and at length, not only with the Iraqi military and other authorities, but also with the UN Security Council.

For all these people, the way the world is organised, Peace is NOT good news. Peace is bad business. Peace interferes with long-term plans.

Unless we de-militarise the world, the dialogue to create conflict will always reign over the dialogue to create Peace. In our present system, Peace is created only when the responsible authorities (politicians, diplomats, secret agencies, war industrialists, etc.) have brewed a conflict elsewhere.

What is the point in me telling my eldest child to respect her younger sibling and to 'dialogue' in case of tensions, if at the same time, I also give her a whip, teach her how to use it and how to enjoy using it?

Unless you understand that we must get rid of weapons first, your cries for Peace, Justice and Human Rights will never be heard.

Dear Ahed

Yes, it is a difficult situation and I understand your point of view, but your suffering for your people distorts reality. Firstly, Israelis, citizens at large, have no power over what their government does, like anywhere else in the world. Secondly, Israel, like all small and non-powerful countries, depending on foreign funds, has to do she is as told by the powers. And, the powers of this world have decided the moment to make Israelis and Palestinians live in Peace should not come for a long time.

You say, 'Now France and America, under Israeli pressure, are ordering Syria to evacuate immediately or to face the consequences'.

This means you believe newspapers and politicians. You do not realize that Israel 'has been ordered' to take this position, to help create trouble in the area, to facilitate and speed-up US's invasion of Syria in case they do not go ahead with attacking Iran. Weapon manufactures and Syrian politicians love the tension and fear thus created because it would mean that Syrian Armed Forces must increase their arsenal and military capability.

To the US it does not matter which one comes first, Syria or Iran, as long as they have work for all their generals, commanders, captains, colonels, lieutenants and soldiers, marines and airmen as long as they keep the weapon industrialists happy, as long as they keep control of the world.

Of course the US has some accomplices, associate countries – allies they are called - that also get some of the cake. This is inevitable. If Washington was isolated, they could not do it.

Alberto

6

GOOD FENCES MAKE GOOD NEIGHBOURS

Some years ago, there was an article in the 'World of Science' entitled Good fences make Good neighbours. It claimed researchers found that, 'partial separation with unclear boundaries fosters conflict'. The piece made me feel sick when I read it first and sick now when I recall it. Apart from being very disappointing, the last thing I'd have expected from 'World of Science' is a war-promoting piece of news.

The New England Complex Systems Institute is located in Cambridge, Mass. The whole Boston area, with MIT at the lead, is home to scientists dedicated to create wars in the world. A majority of military contracts, from the US Armed Forces, CIA and FBI, go to scientists in Mass. Not only weapons either, but new materials for uniforms that soldiers will wear in the future, when fighting wars in hot countries or in space, are being developed in Massachussets, USA.

The feature proceeded to give as an example the former Yugoslavia and India. What researchers failed to describe is how well and happily people in different ethnic groups live together, until politicians, forced by their paymasters or controllers, the Church, Banks, Freemasonry, weapon manufacturers, corporate Press, educate – brainwash – societies, to prepare them for war; then organize the war.

Countries big and small, whether occupied by people from the same religion or 30 different religions, live together, have no problem in living in Peace, but they are not allowed to do so. WHO buys the weapons for the Armed Forces? WHO trains and pays Armed Forces personnel? WHO decides 'We'll have a war'? The People????? NEVER !!!!!! Do soldiers follow 'Peoples' instructions'? NEVER. Wars exist because Governments and politicians want them.

Serbs, Croats, Slovenians, Macedonians, lived all together in Peace for many years. Then along comes the US and EU, telling them - and helping them- to separate and that is it: war starts. The US Government follow the Romans' - and the Vatican's - law, 'Divide and Rule'. This is the best way of keeping the War Machine going, making lots of money and increasing their power.

In Britain, the Pakistani and Indian military train in the same schools, spend their study time together, have their meals together, at weekends go to the cinema together, etc, but Governments spend money sending them to train, so that they can go back to their respective countries and kill each other.

Scientists at NECSI should be told to study politicians' minds to see why they are so avid for power and fame. Why are they prepared to corrupt themselves in order to gain fortunes, big and small? We should tell scientists to study WHY politicians and Churches do everything they can, through education, to keep societies divided. Why do scientists not analyse precisely WHY politicians insist on providing an education to children and teenagers that will result in them being violent, lovers of violence and weapons?

I once read a plea from courageous Sorious Samura, asking Britain and the UN to save his beautiful country, Sierra Leone. I have seen, also, Samura's documentary on the civil war that tore apart his country, full of beautiful people. His innocence was disarming, but did he not realise what was happening to his country was exactly what the UN and many countries wanted.

If there were Peace in the world, the UN, all the diplomats and thousands of staff who work there, the peace keeping forces and many, many other people would be out of a job. Weapons for Peace do not exist. If weapons were not used, it would mean a real, financial catastrophe in the world, because the inhumane humans who run the world have decided that a very good way of providing jobs and creating wealth is the arms business, from large warships to miniscule bullets.

However, there are not enough 'official wars'; this is why arms dealers, manufactures, brokers, have to find cruel dictators to whom they also sell torture instruments made by 'peace loving' countries. They have to create militias, revolutionary armies, terrorists and ordinary criminals, to sell to, otherwise the businesses which include military uniforms, sophisticated communication equipment and all the paraphernalia of war, would go bankrupt.

If any country wishes to save itself, it must think universally, it must try to save also the entire beautiful planet in which we live. We have to understand that if war stops in one country, it only means that a war will erupt somewhere else. Fences, no matter how good, do not make for good neighbours. Arms must be used so that more can be made and sold. If we do not want to see a country torn apart, with all the human and financial misery that it entails, we must stop asking for love and understanding from a power elite who cannot and will not give it.

I could write much more on all of this, but it is time I stopped. My blood is starting to boil.

We must all campaign against arms, not at creating fences, if we want to have a ray of hope of creating a humane world for our children and grandchildren.

Dear Ahed,

Thank you for calling me 'boy'! Believe me, I am not a lawyer. All I am is a seeker of the truth. And in this quest, I shall never give up. I hate arguing, I like dialogue, exchange of ideas.

I am always willing to learn and educate myself, so tell me how I should go about it, as you say that my education is very deficient. We have obviously read different books. You read books that educate and I read books that do not educate. Please send me instructions and I will follow them. I am eager to be an educated person like you.

We'll never agree on what is religion and what is not. To me, all philosophies of life are religions. Now, whether a religion talks of the existence of an almighty being called God, and another talks of the Forces of the Universe involving no God, all religions teach basically the same.

If you believe that religion means a messenger and a book dictated by GOD, well, you are free to believe that, as you obviously like to believe what suits you. It is not really what suits you; it is what you heard from your parents since you could understand language, and it never occurred to you to question the truthfulness of what you heard. Your statement about the wine drunk by Jesus not containing alcohol is new to me. The Old Testament describes plenty of events where everybody was drunk.

The attitude in France, with regard to women covering themselves, is political, not religious, although politicians often talk on behalf of the controlling Church to which they belong.

Best wishes

Alberto

7
ON PEACE MEMORIALS

In the absence of time to write today, I am copying a letter I sent to the **founder of Peace of the World International**, in response to her letter asking for help and support in erecting a Peace Memorial. This should give you an idea of my thoughts and will answer, in part, your question to me: 'What my recommendations to Transcend would be, in order to move forward'.

Dear Sophia Asaviour,

Indeed, I am the musician, but how did you know? Do you like music? Do you play an instrument? Forgive my ignorance, but to which discipline does your title - Doctor - belong?

Without wishing to curtail your enthusiasm, I would like to reiterate that I am not in favour of Peace Memorials. I have lived for 7 years in Geneva, European Headquarters of the UN, where not only monuments, but also whole buildings are created for the purpose of remembering Peace. This is why there is no Peace in the world. It is all Memorial, memory, remembering, something that 'was'. Memorial means something that died and we can now only 'think about it' but we can't do anything, because it is 'dead'.

My years in Geneva and my regular contact with UN authorities, taught me one thing: politics means telling the world what the world wants to hear, but doing the opposite, or whatever accords with the plans of those who run the world. Banks, Press, Churches, oil, gold, copper and leather industrialists, weapon manufacturers, all of them carry out their plans or projects - usually wars - with the help of politicians.

I read about your tragic experience at home and I think you were lucky to be 23 at the time and not 12 or 13, a vulnerable age which could have left you traumatized for life. I congratulate you on founding Peace of the World International.

You say that your responses to life today are the result of having experienced, '*helplessness, violence, pain, tragedy, poverty, aloneness, hunger, fear, sadness, hopelessness*', but I know women and mothers who have had similar experiences and today are politicians provoking or negotiating wars, or women in the Armed Forces, delighted to use weapons and kill.

You say, '*I desire peace like some people desire water.*' But I have the feeling that you do not make the difference between inner Peace and political Peace. You long for, '*not the peace of silence or tranquillity, but the peace of understanding, joy, co-operation, and harmony in a state of contentment*', seemingly oblivious to the fact that this is exactly what causes all the wars in the world. Churches willingly accept they are at war. Politicians are happy building Armed Forces (even un-official mercenary armies), teaching in military schools all the atrocities that we see on television. There is great understanding between Governments and scientists. Almost half a million scientists, in the US, receive their salary from the Military Budget of the Washington Administration. Scientists cooperate with weapon manufacturers, by inventing for them better, more powerful guns, bombs, grenades, landmines, land, sea and air missiles, and so on.

There is great understanding and co-operation between weapon manufacturers, the military and the arms trade, all assisted by diplomats and politicians. For instance, Governments have brainwashed world populations to believe that diplomats are there to solve problems 'diplomatically', meaning 'without violence'. This is the fallacy that allows all Governments to get away with murder. A diplomat represents 'his' country and if he went against the interests of his country, he would be a traitor. For example, the US wanted to invade Iraq, so, the American Ambassador in Iraq's mission was to make sure the invasion could take place, discuss all aspects of the invasion with the Iraqi Government, to the last detail, including the day and time of the start of hostilities.

All wars in the world exist for the same reason, this brilliant understanding, harmony and cooperation between the various fighting parties. And they are all, as you say, in a 'state of contentment'. The rich become richer and more powerful. Why do you think former British Prime Minister Tony Blair and President Bush are always smiling? Because this extraordinary understanding, cooperation and harmony between them, made them super rich.

I am interested in Peace, which for me translates into 'Non-Violence' and I cannot see how this can be achieved unless we rid the world of Armed Forces and, of course, of weapons.

Weapons for Peace do not exist. Weapons are only for killing. If Armed Forces existed as a deterrent only, we could now close all weapon factories of the world, stop building air fighters, warships, bombs, as all countries are already armed. But this is not deemed possible, because it would create mass world un-employment, so we must go on making weapons.

This means communicating with Church leaders and political leaders in all corners of the world to see where wars, big and small, can be staged. Banks are there ready to finance all these activities. It is their main business. Not only wars, but anything that will create violence and the use of weapons, street riots, big strikes, internal revolutions, guerrilla movements, terrorism and mafias. Governments thrive on the business all these activities bring to them. The benefit - commissions or bribes - often go directly to the Bank account or pocket of the politicians or Church authorities involved.

To cut a long letter short, my interest lies in educating people, in making them think and 'understand' why we cannot have a world at Peace, and study together how we can create a new economic system for the world, that will not depend on the weapon business.

At the moment, around 80% of money donations to political parties come from the weapon industry. This means politicians have 'No Option' but to make wars, to help their supporters. Otherwise donors would be asking for their money back!

With regard to Human Rights in the world, I would say, 'this is exactly how the UN wants it to be'. If Human Rights were respected, the High Commissioner for Human Rights at the UN would be out of a job. Of course there are serious and less serious Human Rights abuses, but that's not the point. The point is that, as with all matters political, we should spend our energies in enlightening the world, in teaching them how to read into a politician's mind, how to interpret their words.

We should also teach people to interpret newspapers or anything that comes via the media. The purpose of a TV station showing one piece of news and not another. The purpose of one newspaper presenting some facts in a positive light, whilst another publication will say the opposite.

To your paragraph, *'Let me and others go to this place where there are little or no human rights and build a monument to peace that addresses several basic needs of the humans right in their midst. But, first I must ask permission from someone. Do I ask those who are denying rights? And when they grant permission, what is that saying? Is their 'yes' a positive in the direction of offering human rights?'*

I answer:
We must educate people to understand that the 'direction' is almost always the opposite from what it appears. In so many countries in the world, Governments are happy to see people demonstrate in the streets, in front of Government buildings, etc, because this keeps populations believing they live in a democracy, which in turn allows Governments to do what they want.

You write, *'Ethnic clashes, which first broke out in 1991, have emerged as one of the most serious human rights issues in Kenya.'*

But Governments welcome these 'ethnic clashes'. Kenya is composed of approximately forty different ethnic groups made up mainly of the Kikuyu (21 percent), the Luhya (14 percent) and Luo (13 percent). Other smaller ethnic groups include Kamba, Kalenjin (Moi's tribe), Kisii, Meru, Maasai, Turkana and Teso, who, together with immigrant settlers such as Indians, Arabs and Europeans, constitute the rest of the population. This makes it so easy for churches and politicians to practice what the Romans did to become an Empire: 'Divide and rule'.

You write, '*Most of the ethnic clashes have taken place in the Rift Valley, Nyanza and Western provinces and result from long-standing land disputes among the different tribes living in the region. There is a fear that these ethnic clashes are politically motivated and supported by government and KANU officials.*

Cases of torture, poor prison and police cell conditions, police brutality, unlawful arrests and detention, rape, and abuse of women are rampant. Although freedom of the press is constitutionally guaranteed, and independent newspapers and electronic media operate, the government has often arrested and detained journalists or seized news publications. The government has also been accused of using the courts to deny freedom to political opponents, charging them in court with unbailable offences, even if the evidence adduced lacks credibility.

The economic and social conditions in Kenya are worsening.

Inflation and unemployment are on the rise, and many people are having increasing difficulty living under the harsh economic conditions imposed by a structural adjustment programme intended to revive the economy' and you end up saying*: 'But this is now 2007',* as if the above description belonged to the past. The description you gave is as valid today as ever.

You ask, *'What would you advise the State do in regard to bringing harmony between the **ethnic groups?'*** My reply would be: 'I hope you understand there is no harmony between the ethnic groups, because foreign powers, as well as the Kenyan Authorities, want it this way. Only by continuing with this situation, they continue to make money'. I would also say, 'Kenyan ethnic divisions inspire other countries to do the same.' I would also make citizens aware of local people working, 'spying', for the US and other powers, to make sure trouble is created. I would also say, 'Look for CIA people, often disguised as diplomats, engineers, oil workers, teachers, who are in reality doing a subtle spying job, promoting divisions and violence.' Finally, I would tell Truth and Peace Seekers, 'Look closely at politicians in power, military in power, Defence Ministers, political advisors and see how much money they make out of divisions and clashes.'

You say, '*We at Peace of the World International are engaging others through our commitment to Peace and positive action for the sake of the children of the world.*' But what are you doing to make sure the children of the world are not taught history the way it is taught today? They are brainwashed in order to develop nationalistic and patriotic feelings and ideas, until they are 'ready to die for their country'. What will you do to stop religions teaching children 'our religion is the correct one, others are wrong'? Will you stop schools teaching children to admire 'military heroes', those who won battles and wars, that is, those who killed the most? What are your plans to stop children from learning to be violent and to love violence through games (many electronic) television and cinema?

What are you doing to stop children from growing into loving military uniforms and weapons, attracted by the glamour of flying a military jet, very high and at great speed and by the thrill of throwing bombs into the middle of cities and towns and killing thousands? What are you doing to change the education of children towards peace rather than patriotic love for war heroes?

To me, this list of 'educational' projects comes long before erecting a monument to Peace. I will erect such monument the day Peace has been achieved.

Dear Ahed,

You pose the question, 'One or two states?'

Most Israelis, if asked to choose between: 1) continuation to the conflict, only enlarged, with bombs sent from Palestine dropping in the centre of Tel Aviv or Jerusalem, killing hundreds and destroying buildings or 2) one state for all, a secular state, with equal rights for all its citizens, all living in peace, without the need of an Army, the majority of the people will choose option two. This is because most Israelis are non-religious.

It would be the same with Palestinians. Religious influence promotes separatism. Of course, I am for the One State solution. I know this will make politicians, bankers, weapon manufacturers and the military very upset, but I do not care.

I work for Peace.

Alberto P.

8

ON POWER

There are many historical events that crop up so regularly in questions to me that I will attempt to clarify a few details on the subject of power.

1) Since 1933 - that is 6 years before WWII, when Hitler was dreaming of power and of making Germany 'finally win' a war, as opposed to the fiasco of WWI, when the British Churchill, a closet anti-Jew, determined to help Hitler, with the full support of the German (in origin) British Royal family, all of them anti-Jewish (except for Prince Phillip's mother) gave Hitler and his Nazi party the necessary material help for Germany to become strong again, and build a big Army, with the best possible armaments of the day.

British Banks, and the famous Jewish-owned Rothschild-Bank, arranged many of the weapon deals. And a former Catholic Bishop of Germany, who did a lot to push Hitler towards his anti-Jewish stance, did everything in his power - via politicians and wealthy families - to be appointed Pope.

He changed his maiden name Pacelli to his 'married to God' name of Pius XII.

The Vatican-controlled Federal Reserve Bank in New York, Prescott Bush and many other powerful Americans, also helped Hitler build his 'military' Empire. Whilst Germany was invading and destroying 'East of Germany' countries, England supported her fully. Anthony Eden, Churchill and countless other important British politicians received regular reports on the slaughter of Jews; they listened and crossed their arms.

War lover Churchill couldn't wait much longer to send his Armed Forces to fight, but Hitler had to be weakened first. So they 'helped' other countries fight Germany, until Germany was sufficiently weak to face Britain.

Vatican machinations to send Jews to their death in German hands is now well documented. This is not even the 'tip of the iceberg' of how WWII was 'built.'

Negotiations also were part of the arrangement between Germany (and other countries) and Switzerland. 'If you allow us to deposit what we loot from the world, we'll not invade Switzerland.'

2) Africa: in Washington I know a Ugandan lawyer who lives there, protected by the Pentagon and CIA, for his role in arranging wars in Africa. He has been brainwashed by the American secret services into firmly believing that the only way forward for African countries, is to stage wars. America needs to sell old weapons in order to replace them for new and more sophisticated ones. They also need wars, anywhere, for the sake of trying new weaponry and as a showcase, to gain new clients.

Politicians, Banks and lawyers negotiate weapon deals, thanks to the 'humanitarian' help from World Bank and IMF. Officially they are given funds to help a country, but 'help' in most cases means money for buying weapons. Just like war criminal and former British Prime Minister Tony Blair today announced (and the US war-promoter, Condoleeza Rice, supports him) that they want to 'help' Palestinians. In 'real' political terms, this means they want Palestine to have a better Army, so that Palestine and Israel can engage in a proper war, without the intervention of other Arabic countries, as it has always been the case.

In Nigeria I have a friend, also a lawyer, whose father was a prominent judge and well involved in Nigerian politics. The name is Mbanefo. You can find books on the family. Reading through the life of the late Sir Louis Nwachukwa Mbanefo, it is obvious to me that foreign powers did everything possible to create all civil wars and massacres that took place in Nigeria.

3) Bosnia: Bosnian, Albanian, Serbian and Croatian people, residing in the heaven of 'neutral' Switzerland, became multi-millionaires, organizing liberation armies and armed conflicts in the region. Of course, thanks to 'promoting' a weapon business, which helps the Helvetic country, they now have official residence in Switzerland.

Now to my summary points:
1) How to create a reason that justifies a war. Britain and the US, competing against each other, have been for years trying to sell about 70 billion dollars of war equipment to Saudi Arabia (the arms broker to the Arab world), so that Israel could invade any country any time. The Saudis were not convinced, so the US and Britain had to think of organising an Israeli invasion somewhere, to prove their

point. They arranged for an Israeli soldier to be kidnapped, as the trigger for a war with Lebanon.

2) How long do we wait before we start?
It is a question of both sides being ready for the fight. Both sides are in constant communication. Of course they first must have the usual parody in front of the cameras, that they're - via diplomacy - trying to avoid the armed conflict.

3) When exactly do we start?
They are prepared for the first shots, once the official announcement is made, that diplomatic negotiations have failed.

4) Who fires the first shot?
This is discussed between the parties.

5) How many towns - and which - will be hit?
This is also a matter of discussion between Government and the military. It all depends on 'how many weapons, vehicles, ammunitions they have got.

6) Up to how many casualties can each side take?
This is determined by hospital capabilities.

7) How many air-fighters, tanks, etc, can the Armed Forces lose?

Depends on how much money they have got in reserve for more vehicles.

8) How much money can we afford for a game of war?

It all depends on so many elements. How much funds can the country spare for war? Is the country fighting another country with the same religion or not? The war between Peru and Equador did not last long because the Vatican did not like Catholics killing each other.

9) When to stop the war.

When you've had enough!!! Or you have no more money.

Andre Gide wrote, *'It is easier to lead men to combat, stirring up their passion, than to restrain them and direct them toward the patient labours of peace.'*

In an innocent way, Gide is encouraging war. It is true, 'stirring up passions' is easy, so WHY not stir them in order to lead men to live in Peace with each other? Gide says, 'restrain them', as if making wars was the decision of the masses.

Sadly, the masses, led by politicians and misled by the media, obey like cattle.

The United Nations **'Challenges for Peace'** is an interesting example. WHY is the world, even after the catastrophe and devastation of two world wars, permanently inhabited by armed conflicts, by countries invading other countries, by civil wars, by revolutions, and unrest?

A few words uttered by Mahatma Gandhi sum it up: *'I object to violence because when it appears to do good, the good is only temporary; the evil it does is permanent.'*

While many look at the United Nations organization as if it were genuinely created to bring Peace, Justice and Human Rights to our world because they look at the written words of the UN Declarations, I look at the world from a very different perspective.

I am not interested in Declarations. I am interested in analysis. For instance, I look at which countries form the UN Security Council. I can then see, almost immediately, WHY those countries are members of the Security Council. I can also see how, from their position, as part of that Council, they can create wars in the world.

To me the words of Johan Galtun, *'A focus on peaceful cultures may bring in the human rights traditions, and the focus on peace structures call upon democratic tradition. Both are useful examples of broader approaches for peace,'* are empty words. The 'people' of all countries have always, until this day, focussed on peace culture. They all want to see Human Rights respected and they all long for Democracy.

However, education never focuses on the personal wishes of 'the people'. It does not educate people into 'seeing and understanding' how their wishes are not respected by those in control of world affairs.

An analysis of the first words of the UN Declaration, show how the UN is a WAR organisation, not interested in PEACE.

Read and re-read the words: **'UN declares the intent to save successive generations from the torment of war, to maintain international peace, to take action against aggression, and to develop friendly relations among nations. It aims at solving the international problems of**

economic, social, cultural, and humanitarian character in addition to promoting and encouraging respect for human rights and fundamental freedoms' and it becomes clear how the UN makes PEACE impossible.

Consider the statement that the **'UN declares the intent to save successive generations from the torment of war.'** They have done this by working day and night on developing weapons, each year more powerful and sophisticated. They have been working at developing the most amazing, almost science-fiction air-fighters, warships and nuclear submarines. The UN promotes the research into material for military clothing that will allow soldiers to fight more comfortably in un-welcome weather conditions (desert and space included). All this can only mean ONE THING. They are only thinking of HOW to create the 'torment of war', not to 'save' people from it.

Is it really **'....to maintain international peace'**? The UN knows VERY WELL that, as Mahatma Gandhi said, weapons only create *'permanent evil'*. Yet, not only do they want every country of the world to be armed, they have their own Armed Forces. It even has the audacity to call its armies '**Peace**

Forces', when it knows very well that ARMS FOR PEACE DO NOT EXIST.

What about the promise '**to take action against aggression**'? What does the UN actually do? It promotes an education (brain-washing, I call it) that creates human divisions, be they geographical, ethnic or religious, so that aggressions can take place. '**Action**' will then be taken. Action means war. Members of the Security Council make sure all finances (and weapons) are in place, for wars to take place.

Look at the new war in November 2008, in Congo. How, in a month of great financial crisis for the world, with many companies bankrupt and employees sacked from their jobs, can Congo afford a Civil War? How come the Armed Forces never sack their personnel, but, on the contrary, are continuously recruiting new members, both men and women?

The UN 'war clique' also suggests its aim is '**...... to develop friendly relations among nations'.** This only means, in UN jargon, for countries to become enemies and have wars, so that Peace Treaties can then be signed.

And what of the claim that **'.....It aims at solving the international problems of economic, social, cultural, and humanitarian character'?** This is done by economically (financially) helping countries have Armed Forces and wars. Rich countries not only help poor countries get armed; they also train foreign armies and give all kind of strategic advice, to make sure armed conflict lasts.

There is more to question. Consider the phrase **'...in addition to promoting and encouraging respect for human rights and fundamental freedoms.'** They may do this, but promote the escape of millions - called refugees - so that the UN can 'look after them'. Another BIG BUSINESS for the UN and its rich members, as well as for politicians or Royal Families of developing countries.

If I had to report on the UN Human Security Report, I would do it only to show what the UN Security Council is. Look at how the number of weapon factories has increased, the increase in the number of workers in the weapon industry, all within the period the report mentions, 1990-2003. It shows that the Report is nothing other than 'blatant lies'

It is said that Peace and conflict are two sides of the same coin. I do not agree with this analysis. If I see a dehydrated person, who needs to drink, it is not the same action to give a bottle of water when a bottle of whisky is desired. Of course, I can give the whisky and say, 'Drink it, it is liquid. That is what you need'. But I would not be helping at all. I may stop the dehydration from progressing, but I could also kill with my help.

Peace does not require a militarised world. War does. They are not the same coin at all.

Dear Ahed

Khalid wrote asking if it was wrong to wish the death of Haman? Hitler? Stalin? Saddam? Sharon?'

I will just take Hitler as an example. He expressed in his book, 'Mein Kampf', written while in prison, after attempting to overthrow the government of Bavaria (1923), his philosophy on the superiority of the Aryan race and the inferiority of Jews, which he wrongly also considered a 'race'.

Nobody in the world attempted to correct him. Britain and the US, in those years, even helped Hitler have the Army, Navy and Air Force he wanted. He was appointed, to the applause of world politicians, Chancellor of Germany in 1933, transforming it from a democratic republic into the totalitarian Third Reich, of which he became leader (Fuehrer) in 1934. He was allowed to build concentration camps, he rearmed the

Rhineland in 1936, annexed Austria and Czechoslovakia and invaded Poland in 1939.

With this he precipitated World War II, for which many other countries were preparing for years.

My dear friends, both you and Khalid, you need to understand that Hitler was only a piece in the game of politics. In international politics, the game that militaries love playing is the game of war.

If Hitler hadn't existed, like Saddam Hussein or Sharon, the powers would have created one - the 'Illuminati', the Bankers of the world - would see to that.

I hope I answered your question clearly enough.

Alberto P.

WAR ON TERROR

9

From a letter to a group of thinkers in Pakistan and Afghanistan.

War on terror is just that: war on terror. It is not 'war on Islam'. There is a war on terror in Spain and in South America, but nobody says it is a 'war on Catholicism'. The real problem, the world over, is not Terror, but who created it. It is created by the same people who say they fight it.

In my humble view, anybody who terrorizes others is a terrorist. And if he kills somebody, he is a murderer. No man has the right to kill another man, except of course, by accident, in self-defence.

Sadly, theistic religions provoke men to behave like animals. We do not need Christians against Muslims or vice-versa. Muslim groups have been killing each other for centuries. It is the same between Christians. Look at Ireland's historical war between Protestant and Catholic Christians, or at the Civil War in Spain where killing was among Catholics.

Terrorism, like all wars in the world, is 'business'. It is the Banks and the weapon manufacturers who benefit the most. Sadly, those who hold important positions in Governments and the Armed Forces, also benefit from this dirty business.

As for calling Pakistan a 'Democracy', it is not accurate. Israel is not a Democracy because it calls itself the 'Jewish' State of Israel. For the same reason, the 'Islamic' Republic of Pakistan is not a Democracy. From the moment certain religious beliefs are forced upon the citizens of a country, that country ceases to be a Democracy.

A Democracy can only exist when religion and state are entirely separate - something that does not exist, except in theory - and people are free to choose what religion they wish to practice.

Proper Democracy does not exist anyway. Governments do what they want, not what the people who voted them into power want. Politicians tend to be more interested in their own pockets or Bank accounts than in working for the people they represent. This happens everywhere in the world, Britain, USA, Switzerland, Russia, etc.

Of course there are wonderful, un-interested politicians, who genuinely wish to work for the masses, but it is the rotten system of bribes and corruption - in most countries of the world - and the need to create a violent society and wars, that prevents these true politicians from performing their noble tasks.

We should start by ridding the world of weapons and the military, supplementing this action with an education that will teach men and women that we are all equal, all human beings born with the same right to live and to be happy. Only and exclusively with an education that teaches 'respect for human life', shall we progress to a better world.

If all the scientists in the world were dedicated to study and research cures for complex diseases, we would have conquered cancer, AIDS, and other major health problems. But 70% of scientists are paid for researching, inventing and testing new, faster and more powerful ways of killing humanity.

If the Armed Forces (and automatically wars) disappeared, the money saved by Governments, could be used to develop their country, create jobs, build factories, hotels, schools, libraries, theatres, cinemas, parks, roads/motorways, sporting centres, and other education and leisure complexes. We could also stop the untimely death of the three million people who die every year in Africa from lack of food and medical care.

Dear Ahed,

Your question, 'And why is Israel the only country allowed to be above all International laws?' shows that perhaps you do not quite follow the workings of the 'international community', especially of the United Nations, a 'club' of businessmen who dictate or decide which countries should become richer or poorer, who should live and who should die. I beg you, I plead with you, please read the 30 articles of the Universal Declaration of Human Rights. You will then see that Israel is only one of the many countries that are allowed to be above all International laws.

If you really understood what the UN stands for, you would clearly see how Israel is 'controlled' by international laws. We live in a world where 'obeying' the law, means doing everything possible to satisfy the Banks of the world. Israel, like Angola for twenty-seven years, like Iraq, India, Pakistan, Afghanistan, Bangladesh, Sri Lanka, Nepal, Indonesia, Sudan, and recently Russia and Georgia, do just that, they obey their money-lenders. Banks love them for it.

In practical terms, this means, practice injustice and organise wars. Whether country against country, civil wars, it does not matter what kind of a war. What matters is that people die. This is a sign that weapons have been used. It is good for business.

Why do you think all big Banks - public and private - have branches in so many countries and fight against each other for a slice of the economy of the countries they are in? If you think they are in those countries to help improve education and health facilities, you are wrong, I am afraid.

Ahed, please understand, I am not defending Israel. Far from it. I just ask you to see Israel as part, a tiny part, of the world machine.

Best wishes,

Alberto

10

TERRORISTS AND SUICIDE BOMBERS

It is said of suicide bombers that they think their way of violence and self-destruction is the only choice left. Either defeat and humiliation or death. Some commentators also claim the behaviour of these bombers is rational. Does it make me an irrational person that I do not go and blow myself up with a bomb in my pocket or around my waist? Violence engenders violence. So, the rationale of committing a violent act means that you agree with more, never ending violence.

The conflict of the West Bank does not depend only on the so-called 'hopelessness' of the suicide bomber. Israel has at its disposal, some say, the world's second most powerful army, ignoring the facts that Russia, England and China come before them in the military race.

And when we ask why does Israel have America at its beck and call, we must understand that America is at the beck and call of any country that is willing to use its weapons, whether bought or given in exchange for oil, gold or drugs. Had

Saddam Hussein never switched his allegiance with Russia, the US would have never attacked.

The strategy is to 'increase hate and fear'. This is why newspapers brainwash us constantly with stories and comments that will do just that, otherwise it not good business for the War Industry. Can you imagine the Catholic papers in Ireland telling their readers what a wonderful man the Head of the Protestant Church of England is? Can you imagine an advert in the Irish Protestant newspaper advertising tourist trips to the Vatican? Have you ever seen a Communist newspaper write about the virtues of Capitalism or vice-versa? Can you imagine, in Hitler's time, a radio station saying nice things about the Jews? Newspapers in England, at the moment, carry daily articles on Muslim terrorists, Muslim terrorist cells, potential Muslim terrorist attacks, nearly every week.

They never mention the Christian terrorists in Italy or South America, because they cannot use them to 'increase hate and fear' in Britain. Christian terrorists are written about in Muslim Albanian newspapers. This is the game.

Look at all that American weaponry in the Philippines, simply because this country not only is willing to buy American weapons, but also to give plenty of space to America, for their military bases.

There is, of course, the problem of an impotent international community, which has failed to give Palestinians justice, many commentators argue. But they **are** trying. Believe me, they are trying, only that it takes time for the international community to forget all the French, Belgian, Italian, German, Japanese, American, and others who died, not only in Israel but in many European countries because of PLO bombs, grenades, landmines and machine-gun attacks. I tell you yet again violence engenders violence. It is an irony that pro-Palestine campaigners want the whole world to know selectively of the atrocities committed by Israel on Palestinians.

Feeding on all of this is the terrorist, the suicide bomber, who is nothing other than a piece in the mechanism of politics. Brainwashed and trained by religious zealots and/or secret agents he is a victim of himself.

So many people consider terrorists as if they were another race or some kind of group that comes from another country or another planet. Those of us within peace forums know and could well teach others, about the history of terrorism. Reading through the original religious/history books, it can clearly be seen how terrorism has been practiced for thousands of years. Well before Islam existed.

People are prejudiced against something because they have been brainwashed but do not realize it. As Hitler said: 'How lucky for rulers that people do not think'. He couldn't believe how easy it was to have almost an entire country change its way of thinking, simply because he had a big voice and knew how to choose his words.

Terrorists are part of the same mafia that controls bomb manufacturing and trading - this includes all those selling –or providing - manuals and ingredients for home bomb making. It also includes the many sadists and perverts in society who are happy when they have convinced someone else to give their life and take with them the life of others.

With all the bomb-making material made available by politicians, the last thing in their mind is Peace. Many 'terrorist' bombs have been planted by the security agents to interrupt the Peace process.

All of this makes weapon manufacturers very happy. They also make Israeli and Palestinian leaders happy, as well as thousands of people abroad. And all these people are a part of the 'population.'

Governments spend much time debating how to catch terrorists and suicide bombers. Most of the policies they come up with will increase the use of violence. Why isn't it proposed that scientists invent bombs of all sizes, shapes and colours, that NEVER explode? And guns that do not allow bullets to come out? Because weapons are for killing and nothing else. Weapons for Peace DO NOT EXIST.

Couldn't scientists invent a method of education that creates politicians and masters of politicians (Churches, Banks, Industries, the Press) who see that wars, revolutions, violence, terrorism, hunger, injustice and the like, lead nowhere? Except, of course, to the making of money.

Stop the research, development, manufacturing and trading of weaponry. Weapons are not a deterrent; their purpose is only to kill. If you do not believe me, ask owners of weapon factories who surely do not want to risk bankruptcy. Promotion of religions, which only divides society, should be stopped. The teaching – or, rather, brainwashing – of patriotism should also be stopped.

Sports should not be used to promote nationalism. Video films designed to create a violence-loving society should be terminated forever. Science fiction films that show non-stop galactic wars should be banned. Futuristic films should only show a loving, caring, happy, peaceful society. Of course they could contain real human stories, of love, lack of love, and individuals with normal or eccentric personalities, but they should be free from rifles, grenades, bombs, cluster bombs, landmines, missiles, mortars, air-fighters, warships and torture equipment. Unless we tell our children, through the message in such films, that our future will be one of Peace, Peace will NEVER come.

The only guns to be seen would be in the hands of the police, and they would only be stun guns used to catch criminals who can run faster than police.

Dear Ahed,

How right you are Ahed!

You are so right and you confirm that I am right too. Precisely 'because' the Shah of Iran was NOT a religious man and he allowed his subjects to dress any way they wanted, women to show their legs, people to drink alcoholic beverages, he - the Shah - was a friend of Israel. As a non-religious man he saw all human beings as equal.

But now, religion dominates Iran and its politicians can only go by religion. Religious teachings in Iran explain that Jews are evil, are not human, are animals, are not to be trusted, but this is not a congenital condition. It is imposed upon Iranians with the subtle encouragement from the US.

And by Jews, Iranians mean that: Jews, all Jews. Not Israelis but Jews anywhere in the world. This is, of course, the 'official' position, necessary for terrorism and conflict creation. Without the brainwashing, anti-Judaism in Iran would not exist.

Every time a bomb kills Jews, be it in Buenos Aires, in Brussels or wherever, people in Iran celebrate it. So please, Ahed, do not tell me again it is political. Religious wars exist since we started to record history. Your denial of history denies the Peace process to succeed.

Look at Kosovo. The newspapers, being on the side of violence and the business of violence, want people to believe it is political and describe the 28 people who died there last week as victims of the fight between Albanians and Serbs. Reality is however, different.

The fight is between the Christian Orthodox and Muslims. Even between Christians (Orthodox and Catholic) the war that Croacia and Serbia held in the early 90's, was only the result of religious tensions. During Tito's presidency, with all its defects, Croatians and Serbs lived happily together without problems. Churches re-opened and war started.

Of course I am not denying the political side of the conflict, but it is much intensified by the fact that opposing sides to the conflict belong to different religions.

Alberto P.

11

FULL SPECTRUM DOMINANCE

Since Eisenhower days and before, the US's goal of achieving 'Full Spectrum Dominance' - by land, sea and air - has never been out of sight. This, they decided, can only be achieved by keeping the world at war, especially making sure Third World countries do not progress and always depend financially on the US. Of course by US, we understand US and its allies, so that they share part of the booty.

If you had a sincere, genuine - and enlightened friend who worked for many years at the US Foreign Office and was involved in foreign policy, you would know what I mean.

If you spoke with people who are sincere, genuine and really want you to know the truth, they would tell you that the US, together with Britain, have and are benefiting from the occupation of Iraq, its destruction and reconstruction.

Four Navy commanders with whom I spoke, admitted that 'whilst we - the military - exist, there will never be peace in the world'. One of them, explaining further, said, 'War means business, good business – politicians cannot make much money without wars. However, they cannot have wars without Armed Forces. We have to kill and be killed for politicians to become rich'.

The occupying forces in Iraq control every inch of the Iraqi borders and have not left a building - private or public - unturned.

How do you think these daily bomb, missile, mortar and gun attacks can happen? Do you think it is Saddam Hussein who armed all citizens of Iraq before he went into hiding, so that they kill each other, Shia and Sunni Muslims, at the same time as they time kill foreign soldiers and workers?

The BIGGEST by far mistake that many commentators made in 2004 was to believe that Bush needed the Christian right wing evangelical vote to get elected and Kerry needed the Jewish organized network to get funds - and votes - to get elected.

What both Bush and Kerry need they already have and will always have: the support of the war industry. And to weapon manufacturers it does not matter where wars take place, as long as they happen. Of course the more violent or longer a war is, the better for business.

Coming back to being elected. Bush did not need any vote, Christian or non-Christian, right or left wing, evangelical or satanical. All he needed was his father, to manipulate again the vote, through his long years of experience with the CIA.

The fact they both - Kerry and Bush - approved the assassination of Yassin and Rantissi, proves my point very clearly. They both knew this would create more trouble and violence. This would mean not only more weapon business but - and especially - more Banking business.

The more a country is at war, the more it has to borrow from Banking institutions. As my Naval Commander friends said, 'War is too good a business for Banks and countries to ignore'.

The UN is also, in a way, run by the Banks of the world. Politicians or diplomats are paid by them. Most countries pay their UN contribution with funds borrowed from Banks.

When people oppose conflict saying that the increased death and injury in the Middle East, both in Israel, Palestine and in

Iraq is terrible, they are oblivious to the fact that death and injury is the LAST concern of Bush or anybody in his shoes.

People do not ask, 'Why do we make weapons, tanks, air-fighters, gun-ships, tanks and the paraphernalia of war?' But they are unhappy when weapons are used. Do people really think they are just toys, decorative items?

Society will never achieve Peace by counting on politicians to produce it. It will be achieved only when we convince all scientists of the world not to work anymore for the war industry - not to develop smarter bombs, pilot-less air-fighters, more accurate missiles launchers. And we will have to convince the millions of workers in weapon factories to strike, unless their factories stop producing weapons and instead, produce bicycles, trains, books, musical instruments, shoes, food, goods to promote a better life for human kind.

We will also have to make a law that the Minister of Education be arrested and kept in prison for many years, if violence in society increases during his term, as this would mean he has not done his job properly. At present, this job is SO political, that a Minister of Education has to make sure children are educated to become lovers of violence, lovers of using weapons, of throwing bombs from the sky.

If in our warring society a Minister of Education encouraged an education that taught children to respect human life, the sacredness of human life, this would not be good for Government policies and business.

There is no democracy in weapons. Bullets are manufactured and sold, to kill people. Ballot or no ballot, it will not make any difference. If Governments say they want peace, why do they buy weapons? Why allow them in any country? To have Armed Forces for promoting 'Peace and Justice for all' is a big CONTRADICTION.

Will we ever understand that 'FIRE ARMS' are for making 'FIRE'? Both sides buy weapons for the purpose of using them. Both Israel and Palestine, for instance, are under contracts. We do not wish to stop the purchasing of weapons by **both** Israel and Palestine, so in order not to see them kill each other, we would have to manage new enemies for each of these peoples.

We must not forget that weapon factories do not just operate in times of war. They are producing new weapons on a non-stop basis. Israel and Palestine are their good clients. In turn, Israel is also a very fertile weapons producer, with excellent clients around the world. They have NO option but to buy and use weapons, as politicians are well treated by these Manufacturers of Death.

Weapons are not for gaining lands. Gaining lands is a side effect, or a collateral of the killing. Weapons are made for killing and nothing else. In fact, when trying to gain new clients, exhibitors at Arms Fairs have to explain how their product kills better than those of rival companies. Such a manufacturer never says, 'If you buy my weapons you will gain more lands'. But, 'With my weapons, you will kill more people'.

But change can come! A better society free from war can be done! We must never lose faith even if we do not see Peace in our lives; at least we would have sown the seeds of enlightenment.

But first, we must dare to know.

Dear Ahed,

Thanks for your message. I am very happy. I am sure we can contribute something to Peace in the World.

As for Mike and Khalid's messages, they show fanaticism. This has made them both dogmatic and insensitive to human life. They seem to lose their temper more at Muslims who drink wine and eat ham than at Muslims who kill.

 I say to you, I never heard you shout so vociferously when Iranians were killing Iraqis or vice versa, or when both countries, with Turkey as well, killed so many Kurds. You never raised an eyebrow when Muslim Pakistanis killed so many Indians, or at the bomb Muslims put in the Moscow underground train that killed so many people.

I find it terrifying that all of these things - and much more - do not appear to merit any comment from fanatical Muslims. Thousands of Muslims killing thousands or millions of innocent people, when Islam, so they say, is very specific with regard to the sanctity of human life. Yet, they insult Muslims just because they enjoy a ham sandwich and a beer.

I find your position absurd, for seekers of Peace, seekers of the Truth. If people were all taught to be free to eat whatever they enjoy, as long as the product is in good condition and they are not allergic to it, if people were free to drink what they like, with or without alcohol, knowing there are limits (quantity-wise) for everything, if couples in love, married or un-married could have sex when they feel like it, without feeling they are committing a sin, humanity would be much happier, and would not be thinking so much of wars.

And couples in love could be any mixture: a Japanese and a Lebanese, a Norwegian and a Palestinian, a French and a Moroccan. Love should have no restrictions. Only then will Peace have a chance.

I must go.

Alberto

12

WE ARE ALL BORN AS PEOPLE

I say it again: race is determined by physical characteristics. In the animal world we use the word 'breed'. For instance a dog can be a labrador, a basset, a spaniel. They are related, the way cheetahs and leopards are. Orientals (Chinese, Koreans and Japanese) have some external characteristics in common. Europeans from North to South, East to West also have some external traits in common. The same goes for Africa and for the rest of the world. All this has nothing to do with religion.

NOBODY in the world can be 'born' a Jew, a Muslim, Catholic, Protestant, Christian Orthodox, Jehovah's Witness, Buddhist, and Methodist. People are born just people, boys and girls.

The world has erroneously mixed up, for centuries, religion with ethnicity, and this had lead to so much confusion. I'll just give you an example. A Muslim couple that cannot have their own children decide to adopt. This child will grow up with a

Muslim education. Had the child been adopted by a Catholic or Jewish family, he would become a Catholic or a Jew, accordingly.

Confusion on the Ethnicity issue comes from the fact that people have been educated to consider Jews as members of a different ethnic group. I know that this is VERY wrong.

When I donate blood in the hospital, there are people of different religions doing the same, yet the receptionist taking information from us does not ask us what religion we practice. This is clear proof that we are all the same ethnic group, the human group.

When the Atlantic Ocean was formed, people were left in separate continents. This is probably why people of Bolivia can look like the people of Tibet. I once heard music from Tibet and Bolivia and they had a lot in common.

Religions are the political parties of the past, parties created for power and control. Parties have their followers and opponents. The same in religion. Same as people can switch allegiance from one political party to another, also people can change religions.

Of course fanatics or fundamentalists do not change their religion; the same applies to political fanatics. Generally speaking, you will see that children and grandchildren of famous politicians remain faithful to the political party represented by their forbears.

It should not be difficult for a non-Jew to marry a Jew, because if the Jew wants to marry the non- Jew, it means that he is not following his religion anyway. A religious Jew would not date a non-Jewish girl in the first place. Same with a Muslim.

What unfortunately happens in our world is that Muslim men are educated to have more respect for women of their own religion. So, for sexual satisfaction and temporary company, they pretend to be in love with a girl from another religion, but in the end leave her to marry one of their own group.

This does not apply to Jews in Israel - men and women - for whom sexual activity is as natural as eating, watching TV or swimming. Muslims on the other hand are different. They are pre-conditioned into marrying a virgin, so no matter how much they love a partner with whom they have a relationship, they'll never marry her.

At this very moment, I know five English women who are desperate. One of them almost committed suicide, because her Muslim lover left her to marry a Muslim woman. Three of the men went away to marry women they had never met, all arranged by their respective parents. That these marriages can be very successful is not my point. I aim to demonstrate the pattern of tradition.

I agree with those, like Dawkins, who say that the Bible is too full of horrible deeds. I do not think there is a science-fiction film with as much horror and violence as the Old Testament with its vengeful God. However, there are some beautiful chapters and from a philosophical, as well as historical point of view, I think the Bible should be read and studied as a great work of literature, poetry and philosophy.

The New Testament of the Bible and the Quran should also be read and studied by all. These books are very important for the study and understanding of social history and social behaviour.

Someone mentioned to me an American-Russian-Jewish friend, who, he said looked the 'stereotypical Jew'. But a 'stereotypical' Jew looks very much like an Arab. In England

I have two friends, one Muslim, one a Jew. They look like brothers of the same mother and father.

We are all born as people and educated into our differences. We must aim to educate to celebrate our differences, happy in the knowledge that we are all born as partners in the human race.

Dear Ahed,

I have friends from Nepal, India and Burma who work in Bahrain. They have to do the jobs that the 'Bahrainese' do not want to do. And although it is true that Hindu and Buddhist people work in Arabic countries, priority is given to Muslims. When you apply for a job in one of those countries, the first question is, 'What religion do you belong to?' In Pakistan it's worse, because being a Pakistani, if you are a Catholic, you also have to do all the jobs - dirty, menial jobs - that the Muslim 'superior' people do not want to do.

In England, families from Arabic countries who rent or buy properties, have Muslim staff to drive their car, take children to school, teach English, and so on, but to sweep the floors, clean the toilets and do the menial tasks, they insist on having Christians. I once knew a Muslim couple from Kenya, who had a Catholic employee from the Philippines. They 'insisted' - only to humiliate her - that the floor had to be swept by hand with short implements that forced her to do all the cleaning on her knees.

The Gulf countries are at war with each other. By 'war' I mean the way they compete with each other. Which country has the tallest building, the biggest or more luxurious hotel, the best airport, more tourists, or the highest foreign investment. The list goes on. For this competition, they depend, on foreigners. As long as rich foreigners come into a country to spend their money or invest, their religion does not matter. They want European or American style buildings, so they need foreign architects.

Local people are also happy to mix with foreigners so that they can freely drink alcoholic beverages without being easily noticed. A friend in Kuwait, with an important role in the Islamic Council, makes his own rules by drinking alcohol in the back of his house, where Muslim visitors do not go.

As to the sentiment that Israelis are welcomed with open arms in many tourist areas in Egypt, I have to say that it is true of tourists of any country in the world, regardless of their nationality, religion, ethnicity or skin colour. The only people who are not welcomed with open arms are the poor tourists, from wherever they come.

This 'modern' life requires that non-Muslims be accepted to work alongside local people. But in Israel it also happens.

I've known three Christian doctors, two French and one American, who had jobs at Israeli Hospitals.

Mention of the 'Islamic Council' reminds me of the Iraqi political Party **SIIC, Supreme Islamic Iraqi Council,** that clearly shows how politics and religion are one and the same thing.

Funny world we live in!!!!

Alberto.

13

COMMUNISM, PREJUDICE AND BELIEF

Communism does not mean hiding the truth. There was nothing to be hidden, as the miserable realities of daily life were present every day in every person's mind and heart. I travelled quite extensively during Communist days, especially in Romania. Believe me, the suffering of its citizens, was ample proof that they knew the truth, their miserable truth.

I have spoken to Russian people in NYC, but I have spoken, more importantly, to Russian people in Russia, both communists and anti-communists. I have also once shared a radio programme with Nathan Sharansky, who spent ten years in a Siberian prison and heard a few things. He also gave me the book he wrote, of his life in communist Russia.

I have helped to take medicines and food to where the Authorities denied such things because they were considered privileges, to which only active members of the Communist Party could have access. I have helped people escape communism. I think I know a thing or two about that era of Eastern Europe history.

A friend said to me, 'They do not know one tenth of what Western Europe knows.' Untrue. They had enough computers and access to Internet and other means of communication to know exactly the same as the rest of the world. Several of my correspondents were in fact in the most remote villages of Russia or other former Soviet Union countries. Four of my piano students came from such places and they undertook long journeys, for bureaucratic and geographical reasons, for their visas, every year, to come to England.

'Simply, the West has sophisticated ways of showing beautiful lies that hide horrible truths,' my friend said. It is true, but the East (from Eastern Europe to Japan), the Middle East, South East Asia, Africa, are fast catching up. I do not lump the West all together. But believe me, globalisation, with its over 700 American military bases in the world has had an effect on countries, has created many similarities, more than they ever had before.

With regard to Canadian and Western Europeans, it is less evident now that the Index on Censorship has been silenced, as to what they can and cannot publish about the US. This because they have had some sponsorship from George Soros, the US loving Hungarian.

And what about journalists who are 'arrested and thrown' into jail if they print the truth? In Latin America, under several regimes, journalists were not arrested and thrown into jail; they were attacked with tremendous violence or simply murdered.

Editors make decisions, but in reality, they also have to follow instructions, which they call 'guidelines'- those of the newspaper boss.

When Classified Information becomes public, after forty or so years, you can discover history as it really happened and compare it with what Governments allowed the Press to publish.

Hypothesising on whether Kennedy did or did not want to depose Castro, is neither here nor there, at this time in history when Castro has announced that he will not seek election again and has handed over the reigns of Government. We need to solve more pressing problems, on which the life or death of millions depend.

Obviously, the long dead Kennedy cannot do much now. But one thing is for certain: as we review history we see that Castro, deposed or not deposed, was not Kennedy's concern. His concern, on behalf of the US Government, was to gain Cuba back and make it again an American colony, as Puerto Rico is to this day.

The CIA is paid by the Washington Administration and has to do what they are told to do. The President cannot directly give the CIA instructions. There are other members of his Cabinet who do this. When Allende was assassinated, it was Kissinger who worked with the CIA, but all with the knowledge of his President.

The CIA are so powerful, they control the press; indeed, the CIA actually has operatives who work for the press, such as at the New York Times, Washington Post, and many other publications. It is a sinister control CIA has over so many politicians, militaries and Press, in the US and abroad.

As for peace workers working for change, who say to me, 'How can we achieve anything positive with so many politically ignorant people?' I reply, 'It is not their fault'. Societies are brainwashed, not only by the Press. Since childhood, in school. History is taught from a patriotic stance. There is no world-view. Truth is a variable commodity.

Journalist friends in the Middle East say to me, 'We need those of you who are in countries where you know the truth to help us'. Sadly, Most people here also do not know the truth. People in the USA certainly do not hear the truth.

In the UK, in fact, millions demanded the resignation of Prime Minister Tony Blair because of the way he lied over Iraq, but at the time, with the assistance of the media, he survived his dreadful lies with glory. The same appears to be the case, over the death of the chemical weapon expert, Professor David Kelly.

How does the CIA continue, you ask? Why should they stop? American citizens pay with their taxes to keep them in place. Remember that US policy is: 'anything goes, as long as it is for the benefit of the US and its citizens'.

In America people like to have big cars and pay little for petrol, so you need the CIA to help control Governments in oil producing countries, to abuse Human Rights, to starve millions to death, so Americans continue to enjoy big cars and cheap gasoline.

Whilst the US Government does not finish with the CIA, while the UN accepts that all countries are entitled to have spies and an 'espionage' network, there is not much we as members of society can do.

There are several Rothchilds and Rockefellers in the world. However, because the American military is the strongest in the world, it makes the US President, whoever is the President at the time, the most powerful and influential leader in the world.

The media brainwashes the American people, as it does in all countries. I watch the news on TV when I want to hear what lies politicians are telling the people.

Kennedy had plans that did not correspond to the plans of many powerful politicians in his country - Lyndon Johnson one of them - so he had to go. I believe the US have never had a true democracy. In fact, I cannot see a true democracy anywhere in the world.

People become apathetic over time. They are not simply stupid and ignorant. They have been intelligently brainwashed.

I have pointed out for many years that the President cannot act against the will, or decisions, of his Government and that the vast majority of the Members of Congress, and the press, are controlled by the elite.

Do you by any chance know of any journalist, American or non-American, who has been physically attacked - killed even - for telling the truth?

Governments classify information for 4 or 5 decades. This is not, as they claim, for security reasons; they do it to conceal their lies. The US government opens up its archives only when 40 years have passed and the subjects there discussed are no longer of concern for National security. The same in Britain, give or take a year.

Concerning the debate on Jews versus non-Jews, the practice of repeating the old adage that Jews feel superior, as God's chosen people, is abhorrent and unhelpful. Such ideas can only brainwash society and alone maintain anti-Judaism.

In the beginning, neither Abraham nor Moses were born Jewish, as Jews did not yet exist. Once a God in the sky was invented or created, things changed. In order to have others follow him, Abraham had no better idea than to tell people God had chosen him to represent him on earth. This way he kept his power. About 80 years after Jesus' death, a group of Jews decided that Jesus was right in wanting that God in the sky to be shared by others. Thus, Christianity was born, using the same God, to whom they added a son, to make it different from the original religious take.

Then came Mohammed. He declared himself the new light sent by the same God, who, he claimed, would now be leading the world. The idea of Jews considering themselves the chosen people is - at most - outdated.

A publisher once said to me, ' *Jews, by and large, hate the Palestinians'*. This is not true at all. Thousands of Jews

DEMAND the devolution of all Palestine and an end to all occupation.

To have demonstrations in the streets of Israel against Sharon, of more than 300,000 people, with some 50,000 of them Palestinians, all screaming for an end to the occupation, shows that it is VERY wrong to assume what anti - Jews claim is accurate. We should be aware of the work of the MANY Jewish - Muslim or Israeli - Palestinian groups working together.

In Israel there are villages built together by Jews and Muslims who live as good neighbours, sharing everything. There is also the Institute for Jewish-Muslim Peace Studies. Conductor Daniel Barenboim and the late Palestinian-American Academic Edward Said have created the West- East Divan Orchestra, formed exclusively of Jewish and Muslim young musicians and has performed with them, both in Palestine and Israel, as well as in many other countries, worldwide. It is really TERRIBLE that by the use of one phrase, 'religious bigots', politicians and the press destroy the work of thousands of Jews who are working for a better world for everybody.

Beliefs, like political beliefs, cannot make your body, your blood, your intelligence, different. Muslims are as Semite as Jews. Prejudice is really SHOCKING and TOTALLY unacceptable. Prejudice is based on lies. Christians are also Semite, because the founders of Christianity were Jews anyway.

Thousands of people (millions in Nigeria) die yearly, because of the system, encouraged by foreign powers not to change. In England, in Nigeria, Iraq, Afghanistan and many other countries, top politicians and millionaire leaders are bribed by the powers so that countries can continue to be abused.

One of the reasons for the Kosovo and Bosnian war was to turn the Balkans into the mess it now is. Also to keep the militaries practicing their favourite activity, trying new weapons, testing new pilots, and keeping the weapon industry happy, so they keep giving huge donations to political parties. Also as part of the US plan to control the area and get closer to achieving 'Full Spectrum Dominance'.

Peace is impossible to achieve whilst we go on manufacturing weapons, selling them and training the military. A world abolition of the Armed Forces as well as a world abolition of weapon factories is the ONLY solution.

Living in the UK, I know what Clinton and his wife did to promote the continuation of the Irish conflict. I also know what Clinton did in Africa and South America. However, I cannot blame them. They were working 'for' the US.

When people refer to the Israeli government as 'Illuminati controlled', I cry, hearing yet another prejudiced and incorrect statement. The Illuminati control all sides. The same Banks that lend money to Israel, lend it to Israel's enemies. There are in the US Christian weapon manufacturers who are anti-Jewish, yet they sell their lethal products to Israel. By the same token, there are Jewish weapon manufacturers who sell to Syria, Iraq, Libya, etc. Business is business.

And back to where I started, Communism. It is said that you can't be Communist if you do not believe in Communism. WHY do you think then, that Communism 'had' to be a dictatorship? The Soviet Union was controlled by 1% of the soviet population, who benefited from the corrupted system. The many people, who, over decades, said they were communists, only said it in order to earn extra cash and benefits for their families. It had nothing to do with belief in Communism philosophy.

Dear Ahed,

Good to hear from you, Ahed I am delighted you accept my position on the need for tolerance. Why do you think so many religious writings have been hidden from the world for centuries and many still are??? Among the documents now un-earthed by searching writers, historians and journalists, there is sufficient evidence to prove how the lust for power was the motor behind all those who created a new religion. The differences that concerned you, Khalid and Mike, are mainly between one group of Muslims and other types.

For instance, a Muslim friend of mine in Tanzania, who considers himself an excellent Muslim, always looking after the poor, and an excellent father and husband, very successful in his work, does not eat pork - but he drinks wine and whisky, like any educated drinker - in moderation - since God, he reasons, created fruits and cereals with the possibility of becoming delicious drinks. It is obvious that He meant humanity to enjoy those drinks. He thanks God for every glass of wine he drinks.

And believe me, my friend will defend the Muslim religion to the end. Of course this man understood that fear of God was necessary to make people stop abusing alcohol. In primitive times, explaining that an excess of alcoholic drink was bad for your liver would have been very difficult.

It is the same with Jews. Climate and the way pigs lived in the past, made the eating of pork unhealthy. Making scientific statements in the days religious dietary laws were established was impossible. Saying the prohibition was 'God's orders' was the way to protection. The same with shellfish. In the heat of the desert, hundreds of years back, these molluscs were deemed poisonous. People did not know that certain species could only be eaten in specific months of the year; people did not have refrigeration or freezers. The only way to stop people from being sick and/or dying from eating poisoned seafood, was by giving them 'God's orders'. Brainwashing people by telling them that it is a sin, punished by God's wrath was necessary.

Why didn't people in Russia or Scandinavia come up with such ideas? Because the weather in these countries provided everyone with a natural fridge-freezer!

Traditionally some religions prohibited incineration, but many dead who practised one of those religions, are today cremated. People move with the times. That's all.

My friend in Tanzania does not drink because he wants to 'fit in', as you say, with society. In fact most people in his circle and his immediate family do not drink. He does not harm anybody.

I must go.

Alberto

14

THE UN-JAILED BOMBER

The Ha'aretz Israel news carried an article in 2004 about a young Haifa resident, Eliran Golan, who was arrested, charged with placing explosives near Arab targets in the northern coastal city after he had prepared explosive devices and placed them in various locations in Haifa, including a mosque. Police presented to the media two suitcases filled with explosives and weapons, allegedly prepared by Eliran Golan. Among the explosives were 16 large bombs ready for use, as well as 18 smaller bombs. According to suspicion, Golan also prepared six improvised nail guns, capable of 'killing human beings.' This story demonstrates exactly what I want to press home to you.

If Israel kept Eliran Golan in prison for the rest of his life, if Israel paid huge compensation to the woman that was hurt by one of his bombs, what would it change? There will always be new Eliran Golans.

I know the official education children in Israel receive and, if on top of the official education, you have your father professionally in IDF, your feelings towards Palestinians and Arabs in general cannot be conducive to Love and Peace. The majority of films young men watch, all with the blessing of the authorities, increase their anti-Palestinianism. Add to that the personal, emotional and psychological problems of the prospective bomber and you have the most lethal combination.

Governments also allow the publication of manuals on bomb making, usable replica bombs of various sizes, nail bombs and any other bomb that the mind of man has devised. Governments also do nothing about instructions on the Internet about bomb making. They could do this. There are strict laws to cover pornography.

You cannot jail a Palestinian bomber when he is dead. Anyway, jailing a bomber does not lead anywhere either, as a new bomber will be created by the system. The law is flawed because it is made by people who have become psychologically sick, who, even if subconsciously, wish to create more trouble and violence.

The only solution is to EDUCATE the young, the Law Makers of the future into a better morality. Only then shall we see a ray of hope. Only someone dedicated to love - and thanks to education - a respect for all human beings, can become a politician for Peace. If leaders of countries are former terrorists, former heads of secret services, former corrupted businessmen, how can the world expect them to defend justice, democracy, peace and human rights?

We are deceiving ourselves if we follow the usual route of imprisonment. Bombers are 'educated' to become bombers, in some cases for years. I know of a man who said he did not want to die – that was before being married and having two children. But his wife knew all along that after the birth of the second child she would become a widow. And so it was. He planned his own suicide bombing for years.

I have talked to social workers that have spoken to parents of suicide bombers. All were thoroughly shocked at what their own son had done, because their son was not in the least interested in politics or was very un-educated, politically speaking. I once worked with a Ghanaian, who was also un-educated but was being trained by PLO to become a terrorist against Israel.

The organisers of suicide bombers do not have the guts to do it themselves. Likewise, with heads of countries. If, when they wish to go to war, they were forced to lead the battle themselves, to be the first to die, there would not be any war at all.

In the case of Palestinian suicide bombers, it is most interesting to note that importers of bomb making ingredients are often Israelis. In the same way, it is most interesting to note that Israel couldn't exist without the oil from Arab countries. As the saying goes, Business is Business. Peace is not on the agenda. It does not make money.

Dear Ahed,

You should try not to confuse the citizens of a country with its politics. Americans are not born anti Arab or anti-Palestine. They are born like you and I and everybody else, with a pure mind and without any position either for or against anybody.

If an American was adopted by a couple from France and raised in Paris, he/she would be more pro-Palestine than pro-Israel.

People are very gullible and tend to think or feel the way their Government educated (brain-washed) them to think or feel.

America has a very strong history of anti-Judaism and strong links with Nazism. However, after World War II, and having become the No. 1 rival - enemy even - of the Soviet Union, it had to 'choose' countries to support.

Had the Soviet Union been a great supporter of Israel and the Jews, the US would have had to become anti-Israel and pro-Arab, pro-Palestinian.

As for the term 'Semite' being used for Jews only, of course you are right, Arabs are also Semites. Unfortunately though, you are in a minority group - I am in the same group -because even Arabs often say they are anti-Semite. Funnily enough, I also know Jews who call themselves anti-Semites. What is in a word!

Politics is a game. We are all victims of those who play it.

Alberto

15

LINES TO A POET

Islam, Judaism, Christianity and Hedonism

I do not write specifically against religions. I write against abuse of Human Rights and how they get inextricably linked with the practice of religions, particularly as children are frequently the unwitting victims.

To me, to force a child to eat this and not to eat that, to force an adult to drink this and not to drink that, to cut a piece of a man's penis or a woman's clitoris without their consent (in the case of Jews a boy is only weeks old so you cannot ask him if he agrees to the operation) is all a disgusting abuse of Human Rights.

Baptism, too, is a tradition that involves abuse of Human Rights. How can a child be forced into a faith by baptism? It is counter-intelligent. The brainwashing of the young human mind is one of the biggest atrocities committed by adult believers. Of course, if after growing, studying and reasoning, a person decides to believe in the doctrine of his/her parents, whatever it is, he/she should be free to do just that.

To me, a child should only be taught to be a good, compassionate, honest, hard working, sincere human being, always ready to help others and able to look after himself. He should be shown all available food and learn to enjoy it. He should be able to decide for himself what he prefers to eat and what does not appeal to his palate. A child should know how dangerous for his health the abuse of certain foods is, foods that could make him obese or harm his liver, perhaps. If a child reacts in a negative way to certain foods or drinks, he should be taught to avoid those or taken to a doctor to see if he is suffering from an allergy.

How much better it would be if Christians, Jews and Muslims, instead of unnecessarily dying of AIDS or having unwanted children, were taught how to enjoy safe sex.

I am asked if I have ever read the Quran. My answer is, yes, several times. Not for the sake of reading it, but as part of my religious studies and analysis. I discuss religion with imams, mullahs, priests and rabbis.

How could a man who appeared in Arabia 1500 years ago rule on modern problems, know scientific facts that scientists were able to discover only recently? If you want to believe Mohammed was illiterate, that is your choice. With the books in his house and the life he led, there is no way I can accept that the prophet was uneducated. Besides, his most important wife, among the many he had – A'ishah – gave him the opportunity to further his education, as well as the financial means to form the army he wanted. An illiterate man could NOT have organised such a perfect army, and practised the sophisticated military strategies used by the Prophet Mohammed. Also, in his life, he had contact with scientists of his time, learnt a lot and, as the intelligent man he was, he deduced things. He personally never claimed to be the ignorant man his followers claim that he was.

I am asked how I define 'spirit' and if I believe in the existence of non-material beings. Spirit is the force of life that animates the body of living things, and yes, when the material body dies, the spirit does not die. For the spirit to live by itself, the body must die first.

So, if I believe in the 'spirit', how come I do not believe in God? Answer: God (or Allah) was never a human being, so I cannot see how he could become a spirit, unless he is the spirit of a dinosaur or some other remote creature that lived on our planet before humans started to appear.

I believe in Forces of the Universe, Forces of Nature, who are there, have **always** been there. To me the Universe is infinite, has no beginning and no end. There is continuous transformation.

It is a very long subject and one that I cannot at this point continue to develop; however, I hope I have said enough to clarify my thinking.

I am also asked if I know 'hedonism'. I answer, yes, and that I am in favour of hedonism, but not in the sense that is often meant. I do believe that 'Pleasure is the Highest Good'. But pleasure, does not necessarily mean food, drink and sex.

Pleasure is also reading a book, listening to music, looking at paintings, sculptures or landscapes, learning and teaching, sports, card-games or chess, travelling, visiting new countries or friends. So many simple pleasures. The rising sun, the new moon, a baby's first smile.

In the same way that the tragedy in the Middle East inspires poets to create beautiful poetry, I dream of the day Peace will have a similar effect. I would be the first one to purchase a book of these poems.

By saying, 'If I have to forego all of my beliefs and everything else that I hold dear to me so that I may enjoy a beer and ham sandwich, just so that I may fit into your world, then I do not want any part of it,' you show me that you confuse 'beliefs' with habits, and above all, that you have fear of God.

I know that that the God you believe in is to be feared. After all he sends these devastating earthquakes, like the one in Ram, Iran, a month ago, killing 50,000 in 20 minutes, more than any man-produced tragedy. But of course I respect you for your beliefs. What I am trying to tell you is something different.

I will illustrate what I mean: for one of my daughter's 5th. birthday - 15 years ago - I had a birthday party with her favourite school friends. Four of them were Muslims, something I did not know before they came.

They had strict instructions from their parents not to eat anything with meat. Pork, because it was pork and other meats, because it would not be Halal. As it turned out, the beef and chicken were Halal, as I am surrounded by Halal butchers. The children did nonetheless eat nothing with chicken or beef, because I had no proof that the meat was Halal. These children are no longer children; they are now 20 years old. They still do not eat pork, but this has nothing to do with their religious beliefs. It is how they were forcibly brought up by their parents. Of course the same goes on among many Jewish people.

Interestingly, because as children, parents did not talk to them about alcoholic drinks, these young people are less influenced in this respect and, though they still eat no pork, they enjoy beer.

As for the countries often mentioned, Qatar, Saudi Arabia, where alcoholic beverages are strictly prohibited from an official point of view, almost everybody drinks whisky, wine, brandy, and beer, as long as they do it in the privacy of their own home. Governments know of the drinks' black market, but do nothing to stop it, as most Government officials also drink. In Iran you can buy vodka in Coca-Cola cans. A friend of mine, when he was the Ambassador in Qatar, told me how Qatar officials were given whisky blended with Coca Cola so that others would only see the colour of Coca Cola and those officials who wanted to have whisky on its own or on the rocks, would come to receptions as early as possible, so as to have their drink before people they knew arrived.

The same thing with sex. Prostitutes in London make a fortune out of Saudi Arabia businessmen and politicians. They come to England to do what they cannot do in their own country. Religions only force people to be false, to lie.

I accept that some people do not drink alcohol, eat pork or have sex because they do not want to, do not like it. But not to do it, because of fear of being punished by God, I find an unacceptable prohibition. Of course I respect those who do not think like me.

I want people to be free and educated to be free.

Dear Ahed,

There is a claim that the Saudis bought the politicians in America. It is not just a claim; it is a fact.

You say, '*With the American behaviour and attitude towards the Arabs/Muslims, I doubt that the author who claimed this was accurate to assume his conclusion.*'

Well, I disagree. To me, the author is very accurate. America's behaviour towards Arabs/Muslims is precisely what maintains the Middle East at war and this IS the aim of the US. If you do not believe me, speak to weapon manufacturers. The millions - billions - poured into America by the Saudis is what counts to America. Money is money; it does not matter whether or not you like the donor or client. The US only wants big money, money to buy power and control.

Saudis also bought a lot during and before the Clinton era, not only from the US and Britain, but also France. This is why US is not friendly with France. They do not like competitors.

Saudi Arabia - and so many other nations in this world - buys weapons not necessarily to attack other nations. How else can so many wars take place in the world, wars fought by poor countries? Saudi Arabia and other nations may not use the weapons themselves; they sell them to countries that will use them. To begin with, if they do not get rid of old stocks they cannot buy new ones. Besides, manufacturers can improve on their products only if these are used.

Do you think terrorist organizations, mercenary armies, guerrilla and mafia groups, those who run children armies, buy their weapons in the open market? No. They buy from countries that do not use what they buy - countries that only buy as an investment - countries that buy to keep the bosses satisfied and also to satisfy themselves in the process.

Alberto

16

ABOUT POLITICIANS

I have said: 'A politician should not receive a cent of his salary until he achieves Peace.' You may ask if that means I would collectively punish those who have not yet succeeded, even though they have tried most sincerely.

We face a paradigm. Politicians are paid, among other things to make sure their country has very good 'Defences' - weapons and Armed Forces. This intrinsically means WARS. Not necessarily in their own country, but wars anywhere in the world that will allow them to keep renewing their stock. So, any politician who says he is working for Peace is deluded.

In a recent meeting of the Ministry for Peace organisation at the British Parliament, the House of Commons, a bilingual (Arabic/Hebrew) Palestinian who runs a school for Muslims, Jews, Christians and Druids, was asked, after his lecture, if, to help his project, he spoke to politicians. He answered: 'Never would I trust politicians!'

The reason for that meeting in Parliament is the campaign I am involved in to create a Ministry for Peace (something somehow similar to what Senator Dennis Kucinich has campaigned for in the US). All politicians present agreed with me when I said, 'Assuming the most Peace Loving politician becomes Minister for Peace, he will be working for the British Government – that is, creating business for his Government, for Her Majesty's Government. If this means exporting 500 million dollars of tanks, bombs, air-fighters, and munitions to various countries, this Peace-loving Minister could never oppose such sale. On the contrary, he must, like his colleagues, put the interests of his country first.'

You could ask how many politicians will become homeless before any campaign for peace ultimately works. Anyway, politicians have many ways of making a living outside of politics. I would answer that I am more concerned with the millions who die or have lives ruined by these politicians' promotion of war and terrorism, of injustice and abuse of Human Rights. I am more concerned with the million children who die worldwide - the majority of them in Africa - because they have no good, clean water or medical care. I am more concerned at the fact that the US now has about 700 military bases in the world, half of them nuclear; I am concerned at how they have encouraged the military model because they need to create enemies to justify their military plans and expenditure. Another concern is horror of nuclearism, so much promoted by the powers.

Of course there is a very subtle methodology in place. Very cleverly, they first convince all countries that they should have nuclear power because it will help them produce cheaper water, electricity and achieve a higher standard of living. Now they argue for nuclearism in the name of Global Warming, somehow bringing eminent environmental thinkers like James Lovelock, known for his Gaia philosophy, on board.

They then train scientists from all those countries in US Universities and make friends with them. Use them later as agents for their countries to purchase from the US what they need for their nuclear programme - Peaceful aims only, of course!! The rest is history. What hypocrisy, what comedy politics is!

If you think that all this just doesn't hold together, just for a moment, as an exercise, I ask you to change the word 'Peace' for 'Silence' and 'War' for 'Music'. We accept that musical instruments are made, that music schools teach people how to play them. We accept the building of concert halls, the formation of orchestras, the existence of Radio stations and TV channels, of CD, of DVDs. Could, then, a politician who did not like Music impose Silence on the people?

Whenever there is a discussion on war, there is always the question, 'Do you really feel that no country should have fought World War II ?!?' I have already answered this, but maybe, my position is difficult to understand.

Some historians say Hitler was 'good for Germany'. Tell that to the dead Jews, and non-Jews from Poland, Russia, America, Britain, Italy, Germany and elsewhere that those millions who died in World War II died for the good of Germany.

I too have referred to Hitler in this way. To anybody who lived in Germany after the defeat and devastation of World War I, Hitler helped those people put the country back on its feet, developing its industry, exporting German technology to the world and giving the workers a standard of living that was the envy of all Europe. My 80 to 85 year old German Jewish friends, who were born, lived, studied and worked in Berlin and elsewhere in Germany can tell you the same. But world powers are not happy with this.

If you like to believe that one man, Hitler, could cause a World War and the deaths of 30 million people - well, that is your right. I shall never attempt to convince you otherwise. That you are wrong is another matter and I sincerely hope one day you will realize it. I am not alone in having this answer to the question of how to bring Peace to the world. The answer is known to all those who have the power. They know very well what to do. Only they do not want to do it. It does not suit them. They prefer to remain rich, or become richer, powerful and hopefully famous, a name in the history of their country, of the world, even if this means killing thousands of their own countrymen through sanctions, wars, disease and hunger.

Remember also the military community. For the military war is their 'game' their 'passion'. They prepare, they train for wars in the same way that a team of footballers prepare their soccer games. Of course there is the actual exercise, the being in shape if you're a sportsman, but also, and most importantly, there is strategy. The same with wars.

Right now I am reading an account of the months prior to World War I. It is about mobilisation, about preparations and discussions between countries, discussions on when to start, who should shoot first, how many dead and wounded are acceptable, how many civilians are at risk. Then discussions move on to which countries to support, which countries will give you more benefits, where is the best alliance.

In our story of war and peace we have to know that, as drugs have to be tested on humans, so, also, do weapons. But I beg you to understand that I have never said that **all** politicians are bad. I refer to the ruthless, ambitious men and women who have reached the top by destroying many, many careers, and with such professionalism that nobody noticed their machiavellian activities. They love power, and very cleverly pretend they work for the electorate when in reality, they work for their big paymasters. These are the big weapon manufactures, big industrialists, owners of big Media organisations, big banks, big Royal families, the Church and important Military Leaders.

There is a fashion now among Church Leaders and politicians to say sorry. Only today, the Australian Prime Minister made an apology for his country's historical and legendary abominable treatment of Aboriginal children. Some years back, Bishop Desmond Tutu initiated the Peace and Reconciliation courts in South Africa to bring some sort of harmony there for its people. A Pope apologised to Jews for the Holocaust.

All too late.

In my opinion, apologies mean nothing. They are only made as a kind of mask or make-up. They are there to cover the true feelings.

Look at Iraq. Officially, several politicians have said sorry for the mess they have made of the whole affair, yet a soldier in England, who was recently interviewed, after receiving a decoration, said how bad he felt that he had not been able to kill all the 25 Iraqis he encountered. (He had killed 18 and arrested 7). A soldier is trained to kill and he knows that the more he kills while avoiding being killed himself, the more chances he has to be promoted, make more money, become a hero and hopefully part of the history of his country. Look at Hitler, Hussein, Peron, Napoleon, Mussolini, Pol Pot, and the many, many others. Had they not killed, killed and killed and ordered others to kill, kill and kill, nobody would be talking about them today. And others, equally criminal, like Churchill, de Gaulle, Eisenhower, and Cromwell are heroes for the wrong reasons. They all enjoyed killing.

Which country in the world has political stability? You can count them with the fingers of one hand. Politicians cannot bring stability to countries. Politicians themselves are as unstable as the economy and the market forces in existence at the time they are in power.

Politicians are all 'amateurs'. Studying Political Sciences does not make you a 'professional' politician, even if you get paid for doing the job.

Constitution or no constitution, democracy or no democracy, any King will always be protected, as he works for the interests of the USA. He has no option, unless he does not mind the same fate of Saddam Hussein and Slobodan Milosevic.

Unless you remember all the time that political stability is not interesting, not good business for the powers, it will be difficult for you to make any progress.

My advice is: stop talking to politicians, stop expecting miracles from them. Talk to the people of Nepal, to everybody in the same way. Stop dividing your society in ethnic or religious groups. Talk to the hearts of the entire nation. Make them feel they are ALL equal as well as equally important. The only way forward is a united nation, united in your hearts, not by treaties, agreements or constitutions.

In London at this time, Boris Johnson has just become Lord Mayor. He promises he is a very special politician, who has the solution to our problems.

Where is the solution, I ask. According to the Evening Standard of the 13th February 2008, Mr Johnson plans to chair the Metropolitan Police Authority. Why and how? Is he a high degree Freemason?

What is so new about Mr. Johnson's policies, when he proposes exactly the same as every other politician, famous or not? He offers to get more police on the streets rather than to reduce the number of youngsters attracted by crime.

He promises to pay for 50 extra police, in addition to the 1,000 promised by his rival Ken Livingstone. There is no talk of reducing the number of criminals or of how to educate children and youth to prevent them becoming criminals. Political talk is always around the subject of money and weapons. More of both for the police, they argue, will reduce crime. This is pure ignorance or stupidity.

Free travel has been removed from young people in London because of high levels of disruptive behaviour. Johnson says that the under 18's will have to 'earn back' their free travel. Why 'earn back'? Why not just 'earn'? These young people should contribute to society first, before they have a right to free travel.

Like all politicians he wants weapon scanners to tackle knife and gun Crime. Like all politicians, he promises to reduce crime in London, without the slightest thought about the increase in knife and gun crime elsewhere. All he is proposing is for knife and gun manufacturers and traders to find new markets. What's new about this?

Why doesn't Boris Johnson become a 'really new' type of politician and arrange for a civilized closure of knife and weapon factories, finding alternative, more constructive work, for all employees?

Mr. Johnson also wants new rape crisis centres, New York style crime maps and 440 more Community Police Officers to patrol buses and Tube trains. This only means one thing: that he believes, under his leadership, London will become even more violent than it is today. All very sad.

Barack Obama has made history, by being the first black man to make it to the leadership of the Democrats, beating Hilary Clinton in the June 2008 Primaries. He was subsequently elected, in November 2008, as the first black President in the USA, with a landslide victory. But recent declarations by Obama on Iran, show clearly what I always say: all parties are part of the same class. A group of people who work for the elite that controls them. In the case of American politicians, it does not matter whether the politician is a Republican or a Democrat; they 'must', at this moment in time, keep the tension and fear in the Middle East, by accusing Iran of preventing peace in the Middle East. Hence Obama's words: 'Iran remains the only threat to Israel'. He is as controlled as Bush !

In 2003, millions of people across the world marched against the war in Iraq. John Harris wrote of it in the Guardian exactly five years later under the heading, 'The day politics stopped working'. He referred to Alistair Campbell's diary where it was recorded that Tony Blair slept badly. By this time, defined as 'Messianic', Blair said, 'I do not seek unpopularity as a badge of honour. But sometimes it is the price of leadership and the cost of conviction.' He is reported to have said to Campbell, 'Even I am a bit worried about this one'.

Yes, I went to the demonstrations. I joined thousands of people - a sea of human beings. However, my main, or shall I say, my only reason for being there, was not to help or support the anti-war campaigners. My mission was to tell the people how they were wasting their time. Politicians and Politics do not work this way, not even in our 'democracy'.

I said to the marchers then and I say it again to my readers now: 'DEMOCRACY DOES NOT EXIST.' It is a fallacy that politicians want us to accept as truth. The Guardian, as a responsible publication, is always claiming to speak the Truth. However, this newspaper does not educate its readers in these fundamental truths.

English playwright and Human Rights campaigner, Harold Pinter, who died in December 2008, knew a thing or two about fundamental truths. In his Nobel Acceptance Speech three years before, he hammered home the stark message that we are surrounded by what he called a 'tapestry of lies'. He used his Nobel Speech to tell the assembled audience - and the world - that the majority of politicians have no interest in truth, fundamental or otherwise. For them, the essential aim is to ensure that they remain in power and that people remain in ignorance of all truth, even the 'truth of their own lives'.

I do not know why the quality media perpetrate the myth that we are a Democracy. Not only in relation to the invasion - and destruction - of Iraq, but in many other instances. Government after Government prove that they do not practice Democracy. Why promote the idea that being free to demonstrate in the streets, walk about town with slogans, criticizing a politician in a newspaper or other media outlets, having elections and voting, means that we live in a Democracy and can effect change? It is wrong, wrong, wrong.

You do not need a military Government or a religiously fanatic Government and politicians to qualify for the title of 'Dictatorship'. All Governments are dictatorships.

However, the way the world is organised, it cannot be otherwise. Governments are themselves the victims of other Dictatorships, above them. Politicians, even if they are 'really ambitious', cannot do what the people or voters want. Not even what they themselves want. They have to do what their 'real' paymasters want. The real paymasters are bankers, Oil and Gold barons, and the main 'users' or 'clients' of Banks, oil and gold. In other words, those involved in the War Industry.

Why doesn't The Guardian write about how Britain and the US nursed, educated and instructed Saddam Hussein, to become the man he became? Why doesn't the Independent explain to the world how easily Saddam Hussein could have been removed from power, without a single shot being heard or seen?

And how can anyone believe the destruction of Iraq, the death of thousands of innocent people, of many British soldiers, was a worry that prevented Tony Blair from sleeping? Thanks to this human tragedy, he became a multi-millionaire.

If it is true that he had a sleepless night, more than one probably, it would not be because he was counting the terrible loss of lives and the cost of war. Tony Blair, like any Prime Minister or President, knew/knows that bombs are made for killing; that bombs, when they explode, cannot distinguish between military or civilian people. So, obviously, the death of innocents was not his concern. Financially, he knew that increasing Britain's debts was not his 'personal' concern.

Tony Blair did not sleep because he was doing other financial calculations: he wanted to know how much money he was going to make out of obeying Washington, the Banks and the War Industry. He wanted to make sure he would make enough to pay for his 4 million pound (£4,000.000) home in Connaught Square and all the other properties he was buying.

There is, however, one sign that Tony Blair is, in the bottom of his heart, a good man. Had he not been a good man, he would have flourished, physically speaking, the way George W. Bush did. But our Tony Blair has aged by at least a decade, in a matter of months. Obviously the millions he made cannot erase his guilt about causing such a human catastrophe, for his country and for the world.

'Political language', said George Orwell, is designed to make lies sound truthful and murder respectable, and to give an appearance of solidity to pure wind.' If we want Peace and Justice we must change our language, our trained thought patterns and think it through anew. We must, above all, stop the philosophy of militarism, which governs our economy and our destiny. And above all, we must redesign the role of the Politician. As I said at the beginning, they should not receive a penny of their salary until they move towards the achievement of peace.

It is recorded that even Adolph Hitler said he wanted Peace. It is not important what these paragons of hate say, what is important is what they do. And what they do is ugly. Most politicians are likely to say they want peace. At least all politicians in power. There is little point in listening to what they say. I tell you, politicians excel in the Art of Lying, or the Art of Pretending. It is Salesmanship.

Read this (from the Peace Conference in Annapolis): 'Bush said Israel and the Palestinians would try to reach an agreement on a treaty and statehood by the end of 2008.' You will agree with me that reaching an agreement, if this is what all parties really want, does not take 13 months. We really have to prepare for terrible things to happen.

And we must listen to politicians with great scepticism, not only on the matter of Peace (and war) but also in every aspect of life. When politicians say they have increased the funding of the National Health Service, you can be sure within months some hospitals will be closing down wards, or cancelling operations.

When politicians say that new laws will benefit the poor, you can be sure there is an increase in the cost of medicines, public transport, or tax that will hit hardest those very poor people the new laws were supposed benefit.

When politicians say they will increase funding for the Police and the number of patrols in the streets, you can be sure they are allowing an ever more liberal attitude to violence and murder on TV and in children games. It also means they are planning new street riots.

When politicians say, 'the economy is looking healthier than ever', you know that a big financial crisis is looming in the horizon.

Unfortunately, the majority of citizens do not analyse politicians' words. Not even political 'analysts' do that. They get side tracked, lost in ideologies and prejudices and just see what they want to see or what they have been trained to see within the existing paradigm. The mendacious language is seldom mentioned except by satirical comedy shows. And the citizenship at large does what the commentators tell them to do; they will say that '...so and so campaigned on a 'Peace' platform....'. And echoed by the press and media generally, the masses believe what they read. Even the politicians seem to believe their own publicity.

Politicians nowadays have a poor standing with ordinary people. The news items of various Member of Parliament fiddling their accounts or giving money to student sons to do next to nothing fill the press and media. Phone-in programmes wonder more about how Peter Hain came to spend more than a hundred thousand pounds on an internal bid for the leadership of his party, instead of looking at the plethora of media coverage and wondering what it is keeping out of the news.

Hitler said, *'How lucky for people in power that the masses* (majority of people) *do not think'*. I use this quotation because it is painfully appropriate, painfully true. But the truth is not that simple. People do think, are 'engineered' to think as true, whatever they are told. The population discuss endlessly the trivia it is fed. We are controlled by it and the politicians will not complain about this as long as they are not the central character in the story.

We need to educate ourselves to question, to look beyond the words of what politicians would have us believe. In other words, we need to learn, understand and wake up.

Dear Ahed

May has just posted the full 'Universal Declaration of Human Rights'. Now everybody in the group will know exactly what I mean when I say – and I have said it many times – that Human Rights abuses have never stopped and in fact there are many UN Member countries where they have never seen a copy of the Declaration. The Declaration is certainly not taught in most member countries.

I have just been writing to Rob about molecular biologists and genes, explaining to him that the first Jews in what is today called Russia did not arrive there from the Middle East. They did, though, bring something from the Middle East to teach them how to become Jewish. Molecular analysis shows that Jews from Eastern Europe have far more in common with other Eastern European people, (regardless of what religion, if any, they practice) than with Jews from the Middle East, Turkey, Northern Africa, etc.

Furthermore, what little difference there is between European Jews and non-Jews, is consistent with differences commonly found in small groups who intermarry and do not allow new blood to become part of that group.

The friend who first told me about the Khazars (a Jew born in Berlin who died, aged 93 a few years ago) gave me quite a lot of material to read. She was a scientist and anthropologist. Her husband was a doctor who had spent his life in genes research.

Anyway, this gene or that gene, what does it matter? We can have Christian, Muslim, Jewish, Hindu or Buddhist genes, but we can all have the same cold, flu, headache, back ache, hay fever, arthritis, cystic fibrosis, asthma, cancer, Aids or heart attacks! We are all born and die in the same way, we all laugh or cry for the same reasons. We all share the 'Genes of Humankind'. Because of your intelligence, sensitivity and wisdom - one day you will come to the knowledge that it is theistic religions that have poisoned humankind.

And as for inspiring hatred and revulsion, the history of the Holocaust has also been told by Christians, even Germans who never approved of Nazism or anti-Semitism. I ask again, what have Jews achieved with all this hatred? 60 years of aggression towards them in Israel and attacks to Jews worldwide, bombs or fires in Jewish Centres, Schools, Embassies and even synagogues. Keeping the Holocaust alive in the memory of the world, means keeping anti-Judaism also present in the same memories.

We need to inspire opposition of any and all kinds of oppression and persecution. All we have to do is teach the Universal Declaration of Human Rights to children and adults who want to learn - showing them how Human Rights are not respected in any country of the world. Oppression and persecution exist both in Palestine and Israel, as well as in the whole of Africa, Indonesia, Pakistan, Afghanistan, Iraq, Iran, UK, USA, China and all countries in Latin America, except Costa Rica, where Armed Forces were abolished 43 years ago, so there is no need to oppress or persecute.

Sadly, though, Governments teach about countries that practice oppression and persecution with the aim of inspiring opposition to the people of that country. In other words, to create divisions.

By the way, Ahed, my conversation with the Ayatollah was via an interpreter, the secretary of the International Islamic Council, from Saudi Arabia.

Alberto

17
HUMAN RIGHTS?

When I hear or read about Human Rights, especially of the UDHR (Universal Declaration of Human Rights), it is as if I am hearing or reading a foreign language I do not know. I understand nothing. Faced with the reality of the world we live in, not a word of the Declaration makes sense to me.

Each one of the 30 articles of the UDHR is violated. In fact I find that, as with all things religious, political and military, the 'Articles' were created, invented, conceived, with one idea in mind: for authority - religious, political and military - to be free to abuse humanity, whilst humanity believes they are being 'looked after' by the authority.

From Article One, where we read: *'All human beings are born free and equal in dignity and rights......should act toward one another on a spirit of brotherhood',* to the last, Article Thirty, about *'Freedom from State or Personal Interference in the Twenty-Nine Aforementioned Rights,'* not a word relates to the 'Human Rights' experienced by the majority of people in this world. It is the same story from Article two to twenty-nine. I list here a few of those Articles:

Freedom from Discrimination

Right to Life, Liberty, Personal Security

Freedom from Slavery

Freedom from Torture and Degrading Treatment

Right of Recognition as a Person before the Law

Right to Equality before the Law

Right to Remedy by Competent Tribunal

Freedom from Arbitrary Arrest and Exile

Right to Fair Public Hearing

Right to be Considered Innocent until Proven Guilty

Freedom from Interference with Privacy, Family, Home and Correspondence.

Right to Free Movement in and out of the Country

Right to Asylum in other Countries from Persecution

Right to a Nationality and the Freedom to Change Nationality

Right to Marriage and Family

Right to Own Property

Freedom of Belief and Religion

Freedom of Opinion and Information

Right of Peaceful Assembly and Association

Right to Participate in Government and in Free Elections

Right to Social Security

Right to Desirable Work and to Join Trade Unions

Right to Rest and Leisure

Right to Adequate Living Standard

Right to Education

Right to Participate in the Cultural Life of Community

Right to a Social Order that Articulates this Document

I will write Article 28 in full: *'Everyone is entitled to a social and international order in which the rights and freedoms set forth in this Declaration can be fully realized'*, and end with the dubious and dangerous Article 29, divided in two sections:

1) *Everyone has duties to the community in which alone the free and full development of his personality is possible.*

2) *In his exercise of his rights and freedoms, everyone shall be subjected only to such limitations as are determined by law solely for the purpose of securing due recognition and respect for the rights and freedoms of others and of meeting the just requirements of morality, public order and the general welfare in a democratic society.*

While intending to list a few examples, I have, in the end, listed them all for I could not see where to stop! Each of the Articles is relevant to what I wish to communicate. Each of the Articles is violated every day. Unfortunately I do not have space to analyse all of these Articles one by one, but I can safely tell you that the UDHR was designed to make sure religions continue to create wars, that Third World countries remain in the Third World, that poverty and dependence is never eradicated and that the military complex is 'permanently at work', as well as becoming more powerful and controlling.

The same applies to the Charter of the United Nations, signed in San Francisco on 26th June 1945, and its Statute of the International Court of Justice. Reading just through Chapter Five, on The Security Council or Chapter Nine, on International Economic and Social Co-operation, it is so obvious that all these 'laws, rules and recommendations' are meant to maintain an un-even, un-fair world, where poverty, hunger will NEVER be eradicated, so that the rich and powerful can remain so.

I could write non-stop for five years about the United Nations, who I call United Necrologists, for the deaths they create worldwide. And what a fallacy the High Commission for Human Rights is, as well as what the High Commission for Refugees represents. Due to lack of time, I will just repeat now the words uttered to me by a good friend who worked for two years as the personal assistant to a High Commissioner for Refugees. This friend said, ' *I can tell you that all this organisation does is, to create refugees'. 'They seem to work in partnership with the main body, helping them promote injustice, hunger, illness, religious and ethnic violence, in other words, wars.'*

I have always maintained, ever since my days in Geneva, that the 'only' way the High Commissioner for Refugees could happily perform his duties was by making sure 'refugees' were created.

In my days in Geneva I observed the same in the Human Rights Commission. As the years passed, I could see how the 'Abuse of Human Rights' was on the increase. In fact, it became clear to me that every time a new High Commissioner for Human Rights was appointed, new and more Human Rights were abused.

This is, in brief, why I call the UN, 'United Necrologists'. To me, they are the creators of Death. I firmly believe that the more we invoke the United Nations, the more we praise, respect and promote the United Nations, the more we advance towards a new world catastrophe. The League of Nations, harbinger of the United Nations, did not prevent World War II, did it?

Dear Ahed

You rightly say 'Nationalism is most certainly the scourge of Civilization,' yet you go on to defend the idea of a 'two state' solution. So why do you want two states? This is precisely what the powers want. This is what Bush was discussing with Arab leaders when they met in Egypt a few months ago. And this is what was later happening at the International Arms Fair in London - manufacturers trying desperately to sell weapons to the Arab world, or ask them to broker the deals for a future Palestine.

Once you have the 2 states, Palestine will have an Army to match the Israeli Army, so the two countries will be able to happily enter into a proper game of war. Hundreds will be dying by the day. Is this what you really want? You happily write – obviously because of your state of anger, 'Give us some time to kill them', totally ignoring the fact that retaliation leads nowhere, that killing brings more killing.

As to what Sharon wants, Ahed, I couldn't care less. I shall oppose him or any politician - his initiatives and that of his paymasters' - until the last day of my life, to defend my ideas and ideals.

I shall say everything I think needs to be said, in order to make others see things from a different perspective.

You, and most people, forget that the world is one, that the human race is **one**, and that what happens is the result of communication between the ruling members of this human race. Most people, you included, separate humanity, while the rulers unite in business - business that includes fighting, civil and international wars and starvation. Arab countries are as active as any other in the development of world affairs, in world business. What happens is agreed in advance by all those who influence and control politics, in every country.

Alberto

18

HOPE

Hope? Hope for change? I live within this hope! It is what keeps me going in this endless pursuit for peace in the fullest sense of the word. I am aware that so many have given up on any hope for change, that a hopelessness pervades most cultures, due to the careful brain-washing of political educators, who want people to believe that man is a natural fighter and therefore wars cannot be avoided. What fallacy! Of course, this education is nurtured by religious, political, ethnic and nationalistic divisions. The perfect recipe for the acceptance of war. It is only because of my total conviction that we **can** change the course the world has taken that I say what I say and write what I write.

All my critics say the same: 'Alberto, you CANNOT stop a militarised world', 'you cannot live without Armed Forces'; 'countries must be able to defend themselves'; 'weapons are necessary as deterrents'; 'man is a born fighter and you cannot change him'; 'man is aggressive by nature and wars are a good outlet for their agressivity'; 'there are many people dying because there isn't enough food for all'. It is these kinds of lies that must be addressed.

There will always be violent people in any society, and for those we have the Police, police stations and prisons. I hope to see an end to, to finish with, official murderers, in specially designed uniforms, who get paid handsome salaries, to kill people, all legally. In fact, the more people killed, the better chances of becoming famous, a hero.

Palestinian people quite rightly say that Israeli soldiers are terrorists, but this applies to any soldier, regardless of religion, ethnicity or nationality. However, the 'terrorist' is not the human being. It is the weapon he carries that makes him or her a terrorist.

Every day I hear the question, 'What hope is there?' as if there were no way we can achieve a better world. Of course, whilst we continue the military path, of weapon invention, manufacturing and trade this is the case. 'Trade' equals 'use' and vice versa. One cannot exist without the other. Weapons for self-defence or as a deterrent is a big oxymoron.

Muslim obsession with 'Islamophobia' distorts reality. Look at the catastrophe in Pakistan in the Spring of 2008:Muslims killing Muslims and this has happened since Islam was born. Without going far, look at the fights and killing between Muslims within Palestine. Unless we understand that lack of respect for human life leads nowhere good, unless Muslims educate Muslims to respect the life of other Muslims, we cannot expect people from other religions - who are already full of prejudices and thoroughly brainwashed - to give respect to the Muslim ideals. By the same token, different groups of Christians also kill each other.

Killing destroys hope. Killing does not, indeed, advance the cause of peace. As is often said, it merely increases retaliation and hatred. Sadly, this is 'precisely' the aim of weapons and manufacturers. If weapons did not increase retaliation and hate, if they did not destroy hope, business would be terrible for many scientists, industrialists, oil lords, warlords, weapon manufacturers, bankers, churches and media.

My stance against weapons and the Arms Trade does not stop here. Education is the No1 priority in my programme. It is on education that I pin my hope.

People should be educated to understand that there could be a different world, one without weapons. That is, no air-fighters, no warships, no tanks, no military schools, or military bases, no landmines, no grenades, no 'smart bombs'. Then, there would be no need to educate people into becoming nationalists, patriots, religious or ethnic bigots, fundamentalist zealots, loyalists. Only with such education, would hope and genuine belief in peace be as natural as breathing.

Senator Barack Obama, in the Spring of 2008, battled with Hilary Clinton in the senatorial campaign, both on the hopeful path to the Whitehouse. The first Senator of African ancestry to make a bid for and win the top job, Obama is appealing to the people of America with his dream of reclaiming the 'American Dream'. At the height of the Primary's he published a book called *The Audacity of Hope*. It is a personal narrative in which he speaks of his history and of individual responsibility for education and family as the way forward to stability. His message is one of change, of hope. But, sadly, he has also written on wanting America to become the well-armed Sheriff of the World. Change? What change I wonder!

I have often heard it said that wars help reduce the number of mouths to feed, that they; 'redress the balance'. There is concern that 'a stop to the war industry would mean mass unemployment and world financial collapse'. There is an old adage, oft repeated, that 'the military will go in a natural way; when the time comes, just as Slavery went'.

Well, to all the people who perpetuate such myths, I say - and say loudly - very loudly - 'RUBBISH !!!!' You are wrong. There will be no natural balance until we collectively realise what is the cause of war. When we are educated, we can let natural balance exist. People dying from earthquake, volcanoes, floods or disease is 'natural'. People dying from bombs or bullets is not.

And there is a real basis for my hope. I have observed thousands of people, probably millions, since childhood until the present day, in over 50 countries that I have visited. I have observed how small children, no matter in which country in the world they are, no matter what religion their parents practice, what political tendencies their parents have, no matter what colour their skin is, rich children, poor children, they can all live together, play together, play with each other, love each other, without any problem whatsoever.

I shall never forget a very blond English five-year-old boy who, on the occasion of his birthday, invited his best friend at school, a five-year old girl, to his home. The celebration was happening on a weekday, after school. The boy's mother asked her son: 'In case your friend comes out before you, how will I recognize her?' The boy's reply came. 'She wears a red head-band'. To the mother's surprise, the girl- wearing, as expected, a red headband - was of West Indian origin with very dark skin.

How come the boy never mentioned this detail? It is simply because the boy was born, like ALL CHILDREN IN THE WORLD, without any pre-conceived notion - and prejudice - of skin colour. Fights will occur among children, but this will be the usual and normal childhood fight, even if they all are the same religion, social status or skin colour. Even identical twin brothers can have fights between them. All this is natural. It has nothing to do with the endless pursuit of power and control the 'elite' in this present war- mongering system has.

If the world did not spend on the military machine we would have the necessary resources to feed the world. But not because the money would be spent on the poor and hungry.

Simply, powerful and weapon manufacturing countries would not 'need' to create poverty and hunger. It is appalling to know that social funding is curtailed to buy weapons. For war, there is always enough money. In the US alone, as much is spent funding the military as is spent in total in the remainder of the world. Equally, countries with millions starving have fully equipped Armed Forces.

I hope for a world where wars are not sold to the populations by a series of lies and public relations experts. Wars always make countries less secure. Does anyone feel safer from terrorism following the invasion of Iraq?

I hope also for a world where press barons do not control the information - the propaganda we receive, disseminated as truth. I would like to see a world where there is true democracy – not just the democracy that lets us make a protest in public, but a democracy in which people have a real say. And I hope for a world where politicians are there to serve people and not themselves for the good of the human race, and also wish for a world of continuous co-operation between the 'Left' and the 'Right' because the world view they share is fundamentally the same, despite what politicians want us to believe.

As for religions, I hope for a world of enlightenment, where people learn not to accept it just because they are supposed to. Human Beings are born with the great gift called 'reason'. Well, they should use it also in matters of religion - distinguish what is real and what is fiction.

So many lies have been and are uttered by religious corporations who teach their followers 'not' to lie, that I am not at all surprised we cannot live in Peace – since childhood, I called theistic religions 'the poisons of the world'. I am afraid a long life has only reinforced this view.

Hope drives me to shout about the various issues facing me in the political, religious and Human Rights' forums. I am involved; I could never stop doing this work, which is so important, both for me - and to me. I do hope that what the anthropologist Margaret Mead has said is valid. She wrote: 'Never doubt that a small group of thoughtful, committed citizens can change the world. Indeed, it is the only thing that ever has.'

I am a lay Buddhist practicing the Buddhism of master Nichiren, who lived in Japan in the 13th. Century. To me, this is as close as one can get to the original enlightened man,

Siddartha Gautama, otherwise known as Buddha. This places on me special responsibility for the way I live my life. But it is not Buddhism alone, not chanting alone, that has led me to the conclusions I have reached. Life experience has taught me that we have to educate ourselves to be free of the delusion that the church and state are there for us, for our benefit, even in the twenty first century. We all have to awaken to the reality that knowledge brings.

A Greek friend wrote to me saying, 'I admire you for your courage. Everything you write is so true. I hope that there is still time to change things. Everyday one has to face terrible situations and most of the world seems to be in a state of 'lithargos'' – which, in Greek, means sleep.

For this awakening from 'lithargos', we need education and hope.

Dear Ahed,

God or not God?

I am not trying to be funny, but it really made my childhood so miserable, when my family and teachers were trying to make me believe in God and I suffered so much. Especially after He was depicted as a human, with a face and body like ours. In fact the books told us that God made us to His image. I always felt sorry for God, no parents, no brothers or sisters, no wife or children.

I felt even more unhappy when I was told God is everywhere. So, if he could see both sides of the earth at the same time, I thought, He must be not as depicted to me originally, but a kind of very big thing with many eyes. I used to think perhaps the earth goes through God's body and this is why He could be on both sides at the same time.

I suffered because thinking of the pain inflicted by the Earth going through one's body; very painful for God, I used to think. I sometimes thought of not one body with many eyes, but one body with many heads. As I grew up and read about temperatures in outer space, I suffered, imagining a frozen God. I also started to feel suspicious of His existence when I saw graphic descriptions of God. Firstly, if no one had ever seen God, how did we know he was a man with a long beard? I also wondered how, in outer space, He had obtained the clothes he wore. The more I was told God was spirit and that He had made us in his image, the more I wondered. All my doubts and questioning disappeared the day I realised there was no God who made mankind in his image, but the other way around. Men had made God to their image.

The history of His eternity caused me a lot of anguish. I could see the Earth disappearing one day and I couldn't sleep thinking of a miserable God, who would no longer have us.

I've been dealing with this matter all my life, especially when faced with people who, like you, believe in the existence of such God, even if now many believers accept God not as someone with a human body, but more as an invisible Force.

I accept your belief and respect it, but at the same time, I have to disagree with your dismissal of non-theistic religions. I practice Buddhism and Buddhism is a non-theistic religion with an honourable and valid philosophy.

We'll talk again afterwards. With continuous friendship and best wishes

Alberto

19

PARANOIA, TRUTH AND JOURNALISM

It is not only Jewish journalists who've have been vilifying the Nazis for the last 60 years, but journalists and non-journalists of all religions. And it is not only Jews and Zionists who've been making hundreds of movies and writing thousands of books in this regard, but writers, film directors, film producers and actors from ALL religious denominations.

Germany is not Nazism. I've said this a hundred times. I also know the Israeli holocaust in Gaza and the West Bank has not ended. But journalistic claims that there are 'many many Jews and Zionists around the world firmly standing behind Sharon and his cohorts,' is very incorrect. Those standing behind Sharon are the weapon manufacturers, both in Israel (these I assume are 'mainly' Jews, but Muslims also work in weapon factories) and abroad, where the vast majority are not Jews.

And with reference to the current problems, the war in Iraq, it was not a matter of 'Jews' convincing Bush to go to war, but a matter of an organized group of extremists who have hijacked the American government and their minds in one way or the other. However, those extremists are not necessarily Jewish. They are also Muslims and Christians. They include the scientists working on weapon research and development, who want to see the result of their years of work. Weapon Manufacturers, who need to see their weapons are used and Armed Forces buy more. There are also the Banks which finance or administer all weapon operations and finally, there are the Churches, which thrive on wars. These are the extremists.

I am often asked what would I like the Palestinian people, including Palestinian journalists to do, whilst seeing their own people tormented and killed and watching Palestinian population centres reduced to virtual concentration camps. My answer is always the same: continue the struggle, in a non-violent way. Violence only leads to more violence. Conflict resolution can never be attained by violence. You can see this in Ireland: over 400 years of unnecessary, untimely deaths. 'You killed one of mine so I will kill one of yours.' Can this philosophy and practice lead to Peace?

Recently, a journalist friend advised me to exercise some intellectual honesty. I think that what upset him so much was precisely the fact that I am very honest. He has argued that I am either ignorant or dishonest. Well, ignorant it could be, but dishonest, never.

I want to impress on journalists, too, that the Americans themselves are not vandals. The vandals are Bush, his political accomplices and those for whom they work: weapon manufacturers and Traders. Soldiers are only employees of the State, who are doing a job. If it were not in Iraq, or Afghanistan, it would be another country. That's the life of the military. This is why American Colonel Franks said he would enjoy wars more if he could do freelance work, picking out himself the countries he would like to bomb!

Journalists should not accuse a country, an entire population. The vast majority of Americans are innocent, good people, often too naive to realize the many lies and treacheries with which their politicians bombard them. The same in other countries.

Some journalists have claimed that America killed a million Iraqi children. This is such a gross exaggeration, that I really need to ask these writers what they use as the source. I am in touch with Iraq and with Iraqis in Europe and putting together all the reports and information I have received, I would say that at most, 100,000 have died and that includes both children and adults. Of course 100,000 is also a lot and even if only five children had died it would be five children too many.

The usual procedure for Iraqis is similar to that of the Irish; they calculate a monthly average and this comes to – though it varies a bit from source to source – around 10,000 dead per month. Still an horrendous death toll. Still enough to cause us a chill without the additional numbers added.

We also need to make honest sense of the U.S Financial Aid To Israel: An exhaustive report in 2004 on the Figures, Facts, and Impact of this financial aid showed clearly what I always try to tell you: namely that powers in the US 'want' a Middle East at war. It is part of their sinister plan. They know that war weakens. They want a weak world so that they can control it, dominate it better.

The fortune they gave to Israel is small compared to what they gave, of course over a longer period, to Argentina. And, where is Argentina today? Military coup after military coup, revolution after revolution, bankruptcy, hunger, unemployment.

Who 'ordered' that Argentina fight Britain over the Falklands Islands? Of course, the powers in the US. Stupid Galtieri was so naive as to even say on television that the US had been selling - and prompting the use of - landmines to Argentina and Chile, as a way of 'solving' frontier problems in the Andes Mountains. Many people have already died or been maimed because of this. Of course the US continues in its efforts to force a proper war between Argentina and Chile.

Whilst journalists do not see that the supposed 'help' to Israel is not help at all, there will be not much progress towards a beautiful life of Peace, for ourselves, for our children and grandchildren. Sadly, journalistic writing is not accurate. It is biased most of the time.

It is worth remembering President Bush's address to the world in 2004. You will recall that he declared himself the War President for the World and declared the US Army as the Police of the World.

I love America and its people, but the Washington 'world' Administration, aided by the War Industry, is destroying us all. If it wasn't for Washington, Arafat and Sharon would have danced together in the streets of ONE country, a secular country where people practice whatever religion they wish to practice and they all living happily together.

Comment that the Palestinians (Muslims) were unhappy, during and after World War II with the arrival of Jews is MOST incorrect. These people were unhappy because of the creation –and imposition on them of a Jewish State.

As for inspiring hatred and revulsion, as I have already written to Ahed and repeat here, the 'history' of the Holocaust does just that, whether told by Jews, Christians, or Germans who never approved of Nazism or anti-Semitism. I ask again, what have Jews achieved from all this? Sixty years of aggression towards them in Israel and attacks to Jews worldwide, bombs and fires in Jewish Centres, Schools, Embassies and synagogues.

Journalists' bosses have their agenda, so the writer, in subtle ways, inspires hatred and revulsion of the supposed enemy. To me, journalists would be worthy of their title if they wrote on the Universal Declaration of Human Rights. Children and adults should see how Human Rights are not respected in any country of the world.

Oppression and persecution exists both in Palestine and Israel, as well as in the whole of Africa, Indonesia, Pakistan, Afghanistan, Iraq, Iran, UK, US, China, all countries in Latin America, except Costa Rica, where Armed Forces were abolished 43 years ago, so there is no need to oppress or persecute.

Journalists should never write of oppression and persecution with the aim of inspiring hatred and revulsion of a group of people. This rule must be written in stone and be the paradigm of everyone who writes for the education of the public.

Dear Ahed,

You say, 'I believe in GOD and in my people in Palestine'. However, you continue, 'Right now, the non-violence movement is the strongest choice we have. We do have supporters in this crazy world. We should give PEACE a chance'. BEAUTIFUL WORDS !!!!!!!

These wonderful words show that, like me, Ahed, you believe first and foremost in People. Your supporters come from this 'crazy world'. God does not appear among supporters of Peace.

Alberto P

20

'LEFTIST' QUESTIONS

If you are a 'leftist', you should not spend time, unless you have a lot of it in your hands, reading leftist publications. The only way to form a clearer idea of what the truth is, of reality, is by reading the 'opposition', or, better still, 'all' ideas, from the far left to the far right.

We need to understand the full picture in South America, not just the Leftist side. Of course Hugo Chavez wants to give the wealth of the land back to his people, but not all of it! Chávez is not only a clever and rude politician/ diplomat, he is also a businessman, a military man and is very ambitious.

I am often asked by South Americans, 'Why would this country want Hugo Chavez? And if we do, why does the media say we do not?' The majority of citizens, in any country of the world, will respect a politician who says he's on the side of his people. However, the media does not represent the people; journalists work for the elite that own the media.

Mainstream American media 'has' to trash Chavez and Bush, 'has' to try to get him out of office. Do not forget that the Bush-clan business is oil and Chavez's measures decrease the benefits, the profits of the Bush family business. The US have also opposed right wing foreign Presidents, when things did not look rosy for the American economy.

The US specializes in making the Latin American countries poor, so that they need to ask for help, for loans and be forever indebted to the US. This is also necessary to steal their natural resources and to install US military bases.

Discussing Democracy, a peace seeking leftist friend said to me, 'Switzerland disappoints me.' But all countries in the world are disappointing if you look at them from a 'democracy' point of view. In the US, for instance, you may not need to carry your religious identity, but there are a number of schools and clubs that will not accept Jews.

One learns from lessons. But what kind of a lesson was the Holocaust, for example? To me, many people have learned lessons from the Holocaust. To begin with scientists. They learned to help politicians and the military kill thousands without the need, the bother, the time and the expense of building gas chambers. Scientists developed other, simpler methods of mass destruction. We can now just throw a little something from the air and that is it. Is this progress for you?

I hear complaints all the time about those 'illegal immigrants' and how we should 'build a giant wall on the border', but neither the media nor politicians are interested in 'we'. In fact the NAFTA treaty was signed to specifically open a border with Mexico, to allow the US Government to promote import/export, without specifying 'what'. What actually happens, and for which the Mexican political elite and Catholic Church receive good money, is:

1) The destruction of the Mexican economy, by forcing Mexicans to buy US products but not allowing Mexican products to be exported into the US.

2) The free 'forced' transport of women from Mexico (many from Ciudad Juarez, on the border) to work as prostitutes or become sexual slaves of Washington, CIA, FBI and the Police.

3) The disappearance of many Mexican children, taken into the US for the sex and pornography industry.

4) The easy transport from South America into the US of the second income producer for the Washington Administration, after weapons: Drugs.

Some rightly accuse the US of America of holding up regimes or disliking leaders who, like Hugo Chavez in Venezuela, do not work for the American cause. The US Administration specializes in 'looking for trouble', in 'causing trouble', in creating a situation where they are asked for help, both financial and with advice.

The 'corporate elite' requires that Venezuela have a president like Hugo Chavez. The US creates such a president.

As for thinking that because in Egypt you have to have your religion on your ID it is a negative or un-democratic detail. Think that modern, democratic, developed, neutral Switzerland, also asks for such stupid and undemocratic detail. And how many Jews have I known that had to put 'Protestant' on their naturalisation application forms, in order to be accepted as Swiss citizens.

And when Leftists ask, 'Why do you think we vilified Yasser Arafat?' I ask in reply, 'When did we vilify Arafat?' He was received with all honours at the White House and was made a multi-millionaire by the US (and other countries) in order to maintain an 'un-resolved' Palestinian/Israeli situation. It is critical to read, research and analyse all sides from the extreme right to the extreme left if we are to develop an educated way forward.

Dear Ahed,

You say 'All true religions are clean and their messages almost the same. They are teaching us about justice and some other values.' And obviously for you, religions that do not teach about an Almighty God, a founder of our Universe, is not a true religion and the practitioners of such religion are infidels.

Perhaps you should do some reading on Buddhism. This will clearly show you that what you call 'the teaching of justice and other values', is the same in Buddhism as in all theistic religions. The reason why it is the same, is because religion was created by men and men are all the same. They may vary in skin colour, type of hair, height, degree of intelligence, etc. All this will depend on where they were born, what part of the planet they come from, who their parents are, the DNA they have inherited. Education will come later.

You say, 'The problem is always with the followers and their different ways to practice their religion.' These problems, Ahed, arise even among practitioners of the same religion.

'Each one of us is proud with his religion,' you stress. We are not born proud of our religion; we are taught to be proud. We fear God in such way that we almost have no option other than to accept our own religion as the best. 'We believe in GOD and we are following his orders,' you say.

This is totally incorrect. We are following men's orders. Do you think that God wants some of his children to enjoy pork and wants to deprive other of his children from this experience? Do you think that God wants some of his children to enjoy lobsters, whilst punishing others not to ever enjoy one?

And what about wine, beer and other alcoholic beverages? How can God dictate that some of the world population may drink wine, including in religious services when one is worshipping God and prohibit its consumption to others?

You say Ahed, 'The atheist is an infidel'. But I say to you: the man who steals, uses violence, kills, lies, cheats, hates, is an infidel. And the prisons of the world are full of them, be they Jews, Christians or Muslims.

Look at the contrast, in Japan. 98% of the prison population practices a theistic religion and only 2% are Buddhists.

'The Western media is misleading all of you with terrible false news about Islam,' you tell me. But, Ahed, the Western media slanders Islam in the same way that the Eastern media slanders Christianity. Do not forget that religions are like political parties. The opponent or rival is always slandered. When the Press writes about, say, a crook that was sent to jail, if that crook happens to be Christian, Jewish or Muslim, the religion of the crook - or if the crook has no religion - his belief system is never mentioned.

Alberto

21

WHOSE CHILD IS THIS?

Anthony Marsella, Ph.D is the President of Psychologists for Social Responsibility. I have an email from him saying that for the past two years, he has sent out an attachment entitled 'Whose Child Is This?' to his colleagues, friends, and strangers across the world in an effort to call attention to the horrors of war and to the endless legacy of hate that wars engender.

'I share this attachment with you once again', he wrote, 'at this time of year as we celebrate the birth of a child in Bethlehem 2000 years ago. And once again, I ask why we hold in reverence the life of this child, born so long ago, and yet seem so oblivious to the plight of the millions of children who are victims of war in our time.'

I asked him in response, 'Do you send out the same message when we celebrate the birth of Moses, Abraham, Mohammed, Bal´hahulla, or Sidaharta Gautama?

Personally, I would prefer that people stop celebrating the birth of someone whom we are not even 100% sure ever existed. My philosophy is: search for the truth and – this is VERY hard – make people **think**.

I said what I said, because Christianity, as well as all religions, is a permanent proof of how murderous these religious organizations are. To relate Christianity to 'respect for human life', is, to me, a total fallacy, a real oxymoron.

We do not need a belief in a God to learn ethics. Not even Buddhism, which is also a religion, but without a god who made us. And the 10 commandments are utterly un-necessary. They do not teach anything.

A three-year-old child when he unlawfully takes something from a shop or from a friend does not tell anybody about it. A small child who lies does not tell his friends he's been lying. When a child hits another and makes him cry, suffer or bleed, he does not go back to his parents to tell them proudly what he did. He hides from them something that he instinctively knows was the wrong thing to do. On the other hand, when a child gives half of his chocolate to a friend and makes him happy, he wants everybody to know of his good deed.

Definitely, God does NOT teach anything to anybody. On the contrary, with the fallacy that you can misbehave, repent and ask for God's pardon, so many people who believe in God are continuously committing criminal acts. In fact, we can visit prisons, even the ones occupied by the most vicious and dangerous criminals, and they all have chapels, mosques or other forms of Temple to pray to God.

As a 'lay visitor to Police stations', I have met hundreds of criminals, all deep believers in God. In fact two called Mohammed I met, were proud of their murders, because they thought that sharing their name with the Prophet, gave them a special right.

As I have stressed before, I respect anybody who wants to believe in God. But confusing God with Good is wrong. Or, if you relate God to Goodness you must also relate him to Evilness, unless you believe in two Gods, one good and one evil.

There are of course, people who are religious and good people at the same time. But there are also many atheists who are good and honourable people.

I do not speak against religious people. In fact some of my closest friends are religious. I not only have 'lay' religious friends, but also priests of various Christian denominations, rabbis, imams and mullahs.

As I said, I do not speak about people who practice a religion. I speak about religion, in the same way that it was spoken about hundreds, thousands of years ago, as a political, social and economic force.

This is how all religions started. Politics, geography, power, wealth, control of the masses and rivalries determined each religion, each new religion, as it appeared.

The fact that these religions are based on a God in the sky - or wherever you want to place this Entity - on angels, births without sex, resuscitation and disappearance after three days in the grave, on someone who descended all the way from the sky to hand over a tablet with moral instructions that no religion really adheres to, does not make them 'less' political.

They all achieve the same aim: divide humanity, as the basic ancient principle, so loved by Rome teaches, 'Divide and Rule'.

I prefer not to mix up religion with the people who practice it, or I would not have any friends! Often, people who lead political parties use their power and influence to corrupt others and themselves become corrupted. This does not say the millions who support that party are also corrupted.

Dear Ahed

I understood your message to Khalid, but remind you that people follow the leader, so Khalid should try to get Barghouti to stand behind Abbas, and then the Palestinian people will work together.

But my hope is that Khalid will inspire Abbas to negotiate for a one state, all praying to God, the same God, the Creator of the Universe. For those who believe in such God and those who do not believe there is such God, should also live in Peace, all as one loving united family, all children of the same God. Christians will then follow suit and that will be that. The manufacturers of weapons would have to gradually close down their factories. Of course, this is nothing more than a dream. In reality, weapon factories not only do not close. They increase production. So populations have continual brainwashing and continue to fight.

The reports of the numbers at the demonstrations are quite accurate. You have to take into account not only the demonstrators. You have the old people, ill people, and pregnant women, those who cannot leave work but who would like to also demonstrate.

With the American Primaries in full swing again, you will remember our exchanges on the Bush phenomena.

You say, 'The educated Americans were - and still are - against this war in Iraq', but what about the other armed conflicts in the world where US Armed Forces intervene and cause un-interrupted death and devastation? The US not only, as you say, 'have no business being there,' they have no business being anywhere in the world, outside the US.

The US should get rid of its Forces or at least keep them in their own country, to defend themselves if attacked by one or more of the enemies they have themselves created. You say, 'The people know why Bush went for that war,' but I say they **do not** know, otherwise they definitely would not have voted him in for a second term. However, Bush and his clan know very well how to disguise truth from the population.

You say, the invasion of Iraq had 'Nothing to do with Saddam being a bad guy.' Indeed! Saddam **was** a great friend of the US. However as a friend they couldn't attack his country.

They had to make him an enemy, an evil enemy. 'Because', you say, ' who is not in that region?' Ahed, it is not a question of region. Hitler, Mussolini, Mugabe, Allende, Noriega and others like them, were NOT in 'that region', but were also enemies of the US.

'Nothing to do with WMD,' you say. Of course, one would have had to be a child, politically speaking, to have believed this blatant lie.

You say that most Americans 'are hard working people and do not have the chance to educate themselves about Iraq, Islam, 9/11, Israel.' Americans or citizens of all countries in the world are hard working. In Islamic countries people are also hard working and also they do not have the chance to educate themselves about other countries, or about Christianity, Judaism, and even about Islam itself. This is precisely what makes politicians so happy, because they can carry on manipulating the masses, creating conflicts.

It is not exactly as you say that 'They depend on and trust their media to tell them what is on, and what to do.' The problem is that there are as many 'medias' as there are political parties and religions. People are brainwashed by one side of the political/religious spectrum. They do not get to know the other side. 65% of the Americans who opposed the invasion of Iraq did so because they did not like the idea of a possible war 'so close to home'. They believed Iraq was located next to Mexico or nearby our borders. In 1982, when Britain and Argentina went to war over the Falklands Islands, 80% of the British population thought the Islands were somewhere near Scotland or Ireland This explains so clearly how Governments can get away with murder. The majority of voters know nothing about history, geography or politics.

You write, 'Our congress is not less than our media and churches. They just hate Islam and Muslims and they are ready for another approval to fight Syria and Iran.' You could complete the sentence by adding, 'In turn, the Parliament in Pakistan, Indonesia, etc. - hate Christianity and Christians, or Judaism and Jews. This is what the religious leaders and leading politicians create and want: a divided society.

Alberto

22

POLITICS AND RELIGION

Most religions started as political movements. In fact, politicians learnt from them. This is why it is so easy for politicians to pretend one thing when they mean another. Before politicians existed, Armies were fighting on behalf of their Church. Churches became very discredited and put politicians in their stead, so that the world would be duped into believing that Churches, religions, are only interested in the spirit, in spiritual activities.

Massacres and suffering in the world have been created by religions. Go back to ancient history books, of thousands of years back, read the Bible, especially the Old Testament - the bloodiest book ever written. Think of the Islamic invasion of Europe, of the Christian response, the Crusades, the Inquisition, the Holocaust. Look at Israel/Palestine today, at the conflict Serbia/Kosovo, at Kashmir, and many other places, in South East Asia and Africa, where religious divisions are the best excuse for the creation of conflict.

All religions teach respect for people of other religions but at the same time, they teach how 'they have the truth'. This implies automatically that other religions do not teach the truth, that other religions are inferior. The world becomes divided; Peace is impossible and religious leaders, and weapon manufacturers, via their controlled puppets, the politicians, take advantage of these divisions.

Religion is the poison of the world, particularly theistic religions. In Buddhism each person is responsible for his or her own actions and decisions. In theistic religions, everything is done 'in the name of God' and that 'God protects you'. This is as stupid as me giving a gun to each of my children and asking them to have a fight between them, by telling each one of them, 'Kill your sibling; nothing will happen to you, because I protect you'. Believers in God, are conditioned to think that when something ugly happens it is man's fault and when something good, beautiful happens it is God's will. To me, there are two possibilities: either God is both good and nasty at the same time or God has absolutely nothing to do with what happens on earth, whether good or bad. However, there is a third possibility and the one I favour: that God does not exist, but his imagined existence is a very convenient tool we have to justify all kind of good as well as bad actions.

If Yassin had been a Jew or Sharon a Muslim, the killing of Yassin would not have happened in the way it did. Because many in the Israeli Armed Forces are atheists, you can claim that Palestinians who die, do so 'in the hands of the Israelis', but the majority of Palestinians are still practicing Muslim, so for them, Israeli Jews who die, are only fulfilling God's wish.

By separating, as we try so hard to do, State from Religion, we are slowing down the Peace process. Nobody expects his or her political leaders to practice a religion. The most powerful politicians are those who, in the eyes of the masses, are religious. To prove how religious they are, they try to act as God does. They do not listen.

People in Indonesia, Sri Lanka, and Myanmar pray to Allah for a better life and God sends them the tsunami. People in Iran pray to God for some rain, to avoid a catastrophic drought and He sends them earthquakes.

In short, wars in the world mean religious politicians trying to follow God's example.

Evil happens because good people - the vast majority of humanity- do nothing to stop it. What's the purpose of scientists and engineers being paid millions to work on the development of war helicopters, air fighters, warships cannons, landmines, bombs, cluster bombs and so on. What is the point in training pilots to throw down bombs that will hit their target with pinpoint accuracy if we are working for peace?

Why don't we train Hindus (totally vegetarian) in the techniques of cattle farming? Why do not we plant vineyards and develop a wine industry in Iran? It is fertile.

Develop arms, train people to use them and you'll never have Peace. Had a helicopter dropped the bomb outside a Synagogue and killed a Jewish religious leader would that have made a difference? Surely not. Because military helicopters, bombs and the training of pilots in the use of them, have one aim in common and that is: kill, kill and kill.

Palestinians who fight are not doing it because they want to convert Jews to Islam. However, Chief Imams worldwide, especially those dealing with finance and power, would be happier if not only Jews, but all Christians converted to Islam.

We have to be aware of the amount of money, time and effort that goes into planting Muslims in the streets of England, distributing Muslim literature, talking to people, inviting them to lectures, meetings, with the aim of converting them into Islam.

Two politicians of opposing parties can be great friends, dine, go to the theatre or watch a football match together, but they are still political rivals. When Election times come up, they are furious enemies. So it is with religions.

Politicians and religious leaders behave according to the political or religious bigoted education they received. This is why conflict does not resolve anything.

Believe me, theistic religions, which should provide a philosophy to improve life, are destroying the world.

I have seen weapons in many Catholic churches in Latin America. Even the Vatican has arms. I have seen arms in Christian Orthodox Churches and in Mosques in Cyprus, all ready for action. In separating State from Religion, as I have said before, we are slowing down the Peace process.

The Pope has attended Protestant, Jewish and Muslim services. The Archbishop of Canterbury has celebrated mass with the Pope, the Chief Imam of the Muslim Faith in Britain has attended Christian Services at Westminster Abbey and Westminster Cathedral. And what is the end result? War after war. These people run their churches and organisations. They are paid to do a job. Their position is not religious; it is political. President or Prime Minister will justify going to war and destruction of another's country on the basis that he, or she, is working for what is best for the people. Religious leaders must fulfil the same mission.

Politicians and monarchs have always been involved in the choice of Chief for any religion. Any religious man (rabbi, imam or priest) with high aspirations, ambitions within his organisation, must use his Public Relations skills with politicians; otherwise he is doomed to oblivion.

I am not talking about the 'essence of the faith'; I am talking about the 'realities of the faith', of the 'faiths'. We only see the spiritual side of faith, but I look beyond, at the existential reality. I look at top people within each religious organisation dedicated to statistics and accounts. They concentrate on how many temples or synagogues, mosques, churches there are, by how many adherents of the faith has the number increased or decreased in the last year, how much did we receive in donations, how many bibles or Qurans were sold, how many of 'them' died this month, how much money have we made this month from property and other business. The list is endless.

Since time immemorial religions have been involved in invasions, occupations and killings of all sorts. Always made 'in the name of God'.

This is why it all goes wrong. It does not just **appear** to go wrong. It is for real.

I do not describe either religion or politics as if they were unconnected practices. I talk about the 'politics of religion'.

An article in the Daily Telegraph in the spring of 2008 claimed that religious prejudice IS a poison. Wrong. This proposition starts on the wrong foot. The author of the article, Kushwant Singh, is so 'prejudiced' himself, that he inadvertently confirms what I always say, that Religion **is** the poison.

Singh also confirms what I have always said - that Islam never started as a religion, but as a political and military force. Read Singh's own words: *'Muslim armies led by Mohammed triumphed and returned to Mecca as conquerors. By the time Mohammed died in Medina in 632 AD, the Arabian Peninsula was united as a confederacy of different tribes'*. Where is the spiritual religion here, I ask.

We have the same brutal stories in the history of Judaism and Christianity. The same savage stories of invasions and conquerors. If I believed in God, I would plead to him, 'Please God, remove religion from this planet!!!'

Faith is not what does the damage. The politics of faith and greed are. Why, according to the Bible, did the Jews have to kill so many from the days Abraham went to settle in Canaan? Why did so many Christians have to die when Islam decided to conquer Europe? Why did so many Muslims have to die when Catholics declared the Crusades? Why did so many Jews have to die when Catholic declared the Inquisition? Killing, slaughtering of humans existed since long before politicians existed. It is, in fact, taught by God right from the beginning.

In fact, Abraham proved to be more kind than God himself. God did not hesitate for one second when he asked Abraham to kill his own son. What an example to humanity.

Jewish morality condemns state terrorism, whether done by Jews or by others. Islamic morality condemns the killing of innocent civilians as well - whether done by Muslims or by others. But politicians make people forget their morality. If somebody is pointing a gun at me, I am 'terrorized', whether that person is dressed as a civilian or in a military uniform. Governments, on behalf of religion, make us terrorists.

US and British pilots dropping bombs in Iraq and NATO pilots dropping bombs in Kosovo, killing and maiming thousands of innocent people, are all terrorists. Anybody who kills is a terrorist and a murderer, whether he's been instructed by a Government or a private organisation.

Look closely at the religion of those who give instructions to kill, whether members of a government or of a terrorist organization; then look at the religion of the intended victims and you will see clearly what religion does.

You have to understand that all conservative and reactionary religions were, and in many cases still are, political authorities eager to maintain the status quo – one in which religion promotes ritual and formality, rather than dedicate themselves to the happiness of all people. In contrast, I see Buddhism's aim is to place people's happiness at the centre of the teachings. This is the purpose of the Buddhist philosophy – one that puts people first rather than authority.

Dear Ahed

It does not matter how the citizenship voted. What matters now is what business Abbas and his team will start doing with the rest of the world.

You say of Sharon that, 'He cut his ties with Abbas because of one incident'. This is not correct. He cut ties because that is what he wanted. He had to 'create' the incident.

You say, 'The path for peace is way harder than war.' But also, if you stimulate society to be noisy, the path to silence is way harder. So is the path to healthy lungs. It is harder than the path to diseased lungs, if you stimulate people to smoke. The official smoking ban is designed to increase smoking. People are more influenced by actors smoking on screen than by Government bans or warnings. But we do sell tobacco, so we stimulate smoking and lung cancer.

We must sell musical instruments, CDs, hi-fi systems, videos, DVDs, give music schools and concert hall, so we stimulate people to love music. By the same token, if we must sell weapons so, we must stimulate wars. This has nothing to do with how people vote, or which countries have extremists or not.

Abbas, Sharon, Gadaffi, Chirac, Blair, Bush, Putin are all powerless. The people who control, the Bankers, have the key to Peace. If Bush pulled out of Iraq today, he would need to arrange the invasion of another country.

Why I disagree with your statement that 'the West Bank and Gaza may in the future trust each other and then reach an agreement is because the West Bank is the lung for Israel and Tel Aviv, the air for the Palestinians, so that a settlement must be worked out', is because in the future there will be an even bigger conflict, with many weapon manufacturers eagerly awaiting to 'help' Palestine build their proper Armed Forces. Even Israeli weapon merchants will be selling to Palestine.

Ahed, you say, 'Everything in the Arab World is based on lying or twisting the meaning'. But this is universal, my friend. 'Lying and twisting', as you put it, is a reality. It is a pre-requisite to creating conflicts, worldwide.

I understand your explanation about why Bush was elected, but I believe that he won because he is a very obedient warmonger and had a better PR company, a better team of aggressive thinkers and more powerful and corrupted friends than Kerry. Add to this the fact that the majority of voters have no clue about politics.

The path to Peace is indeed harder than the path to War. You are right, Ahed. It is all Business.

Alberto

23

CHILDREN

We do not live in a child-centred world. We have child soldiers, very young children drugging themselves with poisoning glue fumes, slave children working in clothing factories children caring for their siblings where parents are sick or disabled. I am aware that many of the world's children live on the streets, have no education and suffer from stress and depression, just like many an adult. I am aware of the world that we have created for the child and cry at the horror, despair at the way our world abuses the child we should nurture. Others have written of this and will continue to do so.

I write about children to explain why we have wars, why, despite the obvious fact that nobody likes wars, people of all nations tend to think they are inevitable. I am trying to make people understand that with the brainwashing we receive, there could never be peace. Agencies like Amnesty which campaigns for good treatment of prisoners, and other such Agencies, are all working within the paradigm where war is accepted as a 'given'. We need a different way of thinking, a radical change of education, where the accepted 'given' is Peace.

The Government of the UK has made an announcement that children in England must have five hours of education each week related to culture. (Schools in Wales and Scotland are devolved and make their own decisions). It is hard to know what they aim at, given the funding is limited to £15.00 per child per year. But, no matter how much art and culture we teach our children, we will not stop wars because we also teach Patriotism. Both Churchill and Hitler were artists but they also loved wars.

After the announcement that culture would be built into the curriculum, letters started to appear in the press, with people 'shocked' at the increase of the number of hours to be dedicated to culture and the arts in schools. One reader said that culture could not be pushed on teenagers. A teacher said he had got enough to do trying to keep discipline and that most teachers are not keen to take students on trips to concerts or the theatre, due the over-zealous health and safety rules and regulations. A trainee teacher complained there are not enough hours in the week already, to concentrate on the curriculum as it is now. She feared the plan for culture would increase her number of hours at work.

Presidents, Prime Ministers, Popes, Archbishops and Defence Ministers are what they are, think the way they think, because of the education they received as children, at home, at school and in the Church. By this education, I mean brain washing.

To me this is the most crucial point: Everything starts in, is in, the mind of the child. In the same way that men and women are 'programmed' to fight, children could be 'programmed' to live in Peace.

As they grow up, they become more and more influenced by what they have been hearing over the years from adults (especially their parents). This applies to all cultures and societies, rich and poor, traditional and the so-called 'progressive'.

If a child's parents make racist remarks, the child is likely to become a racist. If the parents decide that they do not like

Jews, therefore continuously saying negative things about them, children are likely to become anti-Jewish.

Enlightened parents or teachers can educate their children to respect people of other creeds or skin colour, but in many areas of the world, they work against a convention, where TV demonstrates - through often very violent films- that racism, violence and drugs are normal, acceptable practices. These innocent, un-prejudiced children will gradually become used to violence and stand every chance of becoming racist and violent young people.

Similarly, in a traditional or tribal society, parents can also educate their children to respect the creeds and skin colours of others, but again, a prejudice born of oppression and hatred, will be passed on to the child.

As for Culture in English schools, I'd first need to know what the Government proposes to be able to make a sensible comment. But I do know that so far it has been a disaster. Culture has meant 'more sports'! Imagine that with this philistine Government, the person in charge of the Olympic Games is the 'Culture' Secretary! The usual title is Minister for Culture and Sports. To our dear UK Government, anything that is popular and stops people using their brain is 'CULTURE'.

When school is more geared to examination success than to culture - or education in the wider sense, when the child has had more years of listening - (depending on the household where he lives) - to anti-Jewish, anti-Christian, anti-Muslim remarks, it is obvious that when this child starts to 'think' individually, it will be in the brainwashed paradigm of his 'educators'. In other words, he will conform and think the same way that his peers or parents think.

Guy de Maupassant wrote that 'Patriotism is a kind of religion; it is the egg from which wars are hatched'. At school children are taught nationalism and patriotism, the noblest thing being to 'be prepared to give your life for your country'. The curriculum states that children have to study history. This subject is used primarily to teach children about national heroes - and all societies have their own heroes that we are expected to revere. Those who won many battles, or as I put it, those who were better at killing, are the proclaimed heroes.

Children play with electronic games where the more people killed (virtually) the more chances of being the winner. They watch TV films that show – and teach – violence. They often sit down at home to watch films of non-stop violence with their parents. This 'entertainment' promotes a violent and weapon-accustomed youth. Yet we are perpetually surprised and shocked when young people are involved in gun and knife crime.

Some of these young people may, one day be running the country. By that time, these children would have had enough 'education' to make each one of them think that there is nothing in the world more natural that having Armed Forces and wars. They think of it as the adult human condition. They have learned that there are 'enemies' and that governments save us from our enemies by war and civil control.

Those young people, after university, may enter politics or the world of finance. Some will move into these careers for highly moral reasons. For others, those inveterate 'career' politicians and financiers for whom any party line will do, once they realize the weapon business is fabulous business, both for the country and for their own Bank account, there is no stopping them.

There will be no change for children the world over who are caught up in the horrors of war and trade that has been created by adults in power until the pattern is broken. For example, it was reported in February 2008 that 300 Palestinians, including 32 children were being held prisoner, kidnapped by the Israeli army.

The Media Department of the Nafha Society for Defending the Rights of the Detainees and Human Rights, seems to be as useless in preventing the horror they stand against. The same applies to Amnesty International.

Instead of using time talking about the number of kidnapped children and adults, they should shout about 'why' those children and other people were detained in the first place. For the sake of children everywhere, why don't they explain how and why Israel (in this instance) is helping the UN in its Machiavellian plan?

The Agency reports that the kidnapped children were transferred to an interrogation and detention centre in direct violation to the international law and the Fourth Geneva Convention. They need to say more. Only then will the world understand that 'humanistic laws', with the full approval of our leaders, are made to be violated.

The organization gives us the age of the kidnapped children, the name of the places where abductions, attacks, invasions and arrests took place, plus the number of residents involved. In what way is this report a help to the children held prisoner? It only helps the UN, with its 'war-mongering' members, to see that things are going 'according to plan'.

Increase of tension and hatred between any two peoples is provoked and maintained until all financial and military details are in place. Once both sides are ready, the Game of War starts. Israel has had games of war with several countries in the area but is longing for a good game with Palestine. I do not mean to refer to the people of Israel, who, left alone, would not have any of it. I refer to the politicians in power, who, for the sake of becoming very rich and feeling influential, sell their soul to corruption and greed, whilst millions of innocent Israelis are duped into believing they are fighting a righteous cause. All the many Human Rights organizations do - willingly or not - is to bring forward the conflict.

As I have said, I write about children and their education in both home and school to explain why we have wars. That these children are largely in the so called developed world does not mean I forget the plight of children in poor countries, where education is replaced by work, voluntary or slavery, or soldiering. The situation lays down the fundamental hatred of a world society that allows such injustice. Children will then be 'educated' in prejudice, by parents and teachers who are prejudiced themselves.

In 2008, I was honoured by a Nomination for the Nobel Peace Prize. A child sent me a message saying that he hoped I would get the Award because even he, a school child, knew that a world without war would be a better world. He said that he hoped I would get the Award for the sake of the children in the world. My daily wish is to make people understand that with the brainwashing children receive into the old paradigms, there will never be peace. We must learn the real reasons for wars, to be able to educate ourselves and cause a change.

Dear Ahed,

What you write at the end of your message to me, uttered by your cousin in Ramallah, is true: 'Once you lose your own son/daughter, your own house/property, then you are going to understand why we are very frustrated.' I know these words are true but I also know they are not new and they are not limited to Ramallah or even the whole of Palestine. They are universal.

My own father's family lost all they had, homes, money, jobs, and many relatives, in Romania, Russia, Poland and Lithuania. Also some lost their limbs, arms or legs. My maternal grandmother cried almost every day of her life, since having to abandon her home in Romania during World War II, until the day she died.

In England there are some Cypriots who after 35 or 40 years still do not speak English. They dream, day and night of one day going back to the homes they were forced to abandon, thanks to politicians and two big religious corporations.

England is now full of Bosnians, Macedonians, Croatians, Serbians, Somalis, Afghans, Sudanese and many other nationalities, who all lost their home and family members. Many children saw their own father have his throat cut with a dagger, and die in front of them. These children - adults today - are not only frustrated, but traumatised for life.

You say that you blame the United Nations, America, Canada, West Europe, but this is a contradiction. Why 'West' Europe only, when you also say 'United Nations'. This sinister organisation, the United Nations, is supposed to represent West, Central and East Europe. Indeed, it represents the whole world.

And here is where I feel you fail to see what is happening in Palestine. The whole world permits it to happen, the same way they permitted Pol Pot to kill almost 2 million Cambodians. The whole world permitted - actually promoted - 27 years of Civil War in Angola. The whole world permitted - and created - the many years of Civil War in Lebanon. America, Canada and Western Europe are only part of this 'whole world'. Russian, Chinese, Japanese, Indian, Saudi, Syrian and other Banks, who do are not in 'West Europe', but all of them make the misery of Palestinians possible. And Palestine, as all the Arab countries, is also 'on the side' of the majority UN countries. They are equally responsible - you know it very well - for the miserable life and continuous suffering of the Palestinian people. Arafat became a multi-millionaire for allowing his people to suffer, by obeying universal powers.

Blaming Israel or Jews worldwide is missing the point completely. There are masses of Muslims and Christians who are as much responsible for the Palestinian tragedy, as Jews are, if not more.

Alberto

24

WHY WAR? WHY PALESTINE?

My anguished Palestinian friends constantly ask me, WHY Palestine? Why do the Palestinian people have to suffer so?

The more I think about it, the more I believe these friends should meet some of the millionaire Palestinians in exile. Other millionaires - multi-millionaires. Muslims and Arabs, become friendly with them as well as with the owners of Arab Banks.

These friends need to attend a few 'Arms Fairs', meet Arms traders, arms inventors and their like, and they will finally and forever understand WHY Palestinians suffer the way they do, why Palestinians MUST suffer. Just like the millions who die every year in Africa or the thousands who die every year in South East Asia and Latin America, and other countries, for the same reasons.

They will finally understand that the fate of the Palestinian people has NOTHING TO DO with Israel, with Jews, or with any ideology, for that matter. They will see it has all been created by business - business interests, business transactions, scientific research and experiments with business in mind. There is also Banks' involvement, Media and Church involvement, not to mention business bribes and other payouts.

Unless they see Israel is being 'used' by these groups -and believe me, some of them are Arab and Muslim groups - Palestinians will never understand and will never be able to affect a change.

I am also asked, 'Why do all immigrant children from Ethiopia, for example, have to go to religious schools?' This is again part of the problem: Religious Control. People are not born religious. A religion is imposed upon them. All theistic religions do the same. This is how religious zealots are formed and how the seeds of future wars are planted.

There is no civil marriage in Israel for reasons of control. Israel is defined as a Jewish state – how could it be possible to create the mess and agony in the area otherwise? A great number of Israeli Jews are agnostic or plain atheist. They are totally blind to the fact that Israel is not a democracy.

My friends ask why, if there is separation between synagogue and the state, so many Knesset members are religious Jews, even rabbis?' I will tell them that there is NO separation between Synagogue and State. The Synagogue controls the State and the State controls the Synagogue. They are partners in this enterprise.

'Have you read the history of Europe?' I ask them. 'Do you know the number of Kings and Queens that were assassinated if they did not follow Vatican orders?' This is religion. Why do you think that Prophet Mohammed needed armies? Why couldn't he teach the Quran without invading other countries? Religion and State are never separated.

We must not confuse religion as a political, business and power organisation, with people who belong to this or that religion. These good people do not count, for the purpose of decision-making. Ordinary religious individuals do not think of making war. The bosses or heads do it.

As for Jews calling non-Jews animals, Muslims say the same thing about Jews. I tell you again: 'Nothing is more vicious, dangerous and sinister in the world than organised theistic religion'.

I have been watching Israel for sixty years. The 'Jewish state' is a myth – there is nothing Jewish about it, and for that reason, I cannot agree with people that say Israelis do not want non-Jews in Israel. This is senseless and groundless comment and shows what brainwashing the Press and religious leaders can do.

90% of the Jewish population of Israel is non-religious, non-kosher and couldn't care less whether their neighbours practice Judaism, any other religion or none. Theistic religions are, as I often say, the 'Poison of the World', the cause of most human conflicts. By 'religions' I mean the people who started them, who control them; they divide society, they separate populations, they declare 'other religions' are not good and do not have the Truth.

Present day leaders, in order to try and keep their position and religion 'supreme' have to influence the masses in the same way as the originators of the religion they represent.

You then have the 'business' aspect. Washington and other powers pay vast sums of money to keep the terrible situation going. If Israel does not spend 'x' amount of money on US made weapons, the US help stops. Several Arabic countries are equally involved in 'the business'.

Look at Sudan. You will recall a silly religious matter - a teacher who called a teddy bear Mohammed - was transformed into a wonderful bargaining tool for the Sudanese Government, who said to Britain - of course this did not appear in the Media - 'Sell us lots of weapons for a reasonable price, or we kill the English language teacher'. So, from this minor incident, religion was used to help provoke the next round of Civil War in Sudan.

I have been to Israel; I saw Muslim men and women hug Jewish men and women of all ages and vice-versa. Men and women do not instruct armies to have wars. Instructions come from those in Government, on both sides of the conflict, who, in turn, obey orders from those who command and control them.

I have even known war-mongering Jewish politicians who, when young, were always hanging around with Muslim friends and I have been to a party in a Muslim home of a politician-to-be, where at least 70% of the guests were Jews. But this was, when they were young and genuinely dreaming of changing the world. Once they become well-known, successful politicians, they are no longer masters of their own ideas and plans.

Getting rid of one politician and making space for a new one does not change a thing. It is the 'System' we must change.

Some Palestinian politicians are victims, like so many others, of the manipulations of secret services, who work for the war-mongering Governments at the services of the War Industry. They are all convinced that, given the financial help War Envoy and warmonger Tony Blair is now negotiating, they could arm themselves, could even hire professional warriors and have a good, really good game of war with Israel. This is very BAD news for everybody.

Of course the weapon industry and Banks, as well as several Churches, are all over the moon and looking forward to the slaughter.

We have seen a similar situation going on in Serbia/Kosovo. The Serbian President prefers to avoid a bloodbath and allow Kosovo to become an independent country. We have listened to the Kosovian people celebrating as their new flag is raised. However, the Kosovo Prime Minister, Washington and CIA controlled, is all 'for' war, if necessary. He's been cleverly brain-washed by the secret services, by the Heads of the Orthodox Church, by US diplomats, by arm traders, that 'patriotism' comes first, even if that means thousands dead, that he would show himself to be a bad patriot, if he does not defend 'his' country. That Kosovo 'IS' Serbia and must remain Serbia gets overlooked. I repeat: Very Bad News.

I also repeat: by not opposing weapon research, manufacturing and trade, but on the contrary, making this the BEST BUSINESS possible, we are all promoting human suffering. No Peace Proposal can work whilst we have Armies. Weapons to preserve Peace is an oxymoron. It is as stupid as giving a bottle of whisky to a dying alcoholic who is desperately trying to stop drinking and regain his health.

I am delighted that some brave journalists let people know what abominations Israeli politicians, Jewish religious leaders, Jewish writers have said about Palestine and

Palestinians. I'd suggest now, in the name of Justice, to redress the balance, that they also let people read all the horrible things Muslims have said of Jews (and Christians). People must not forget that it is 'Religions' which are at war, not people. Politicians are merely their 'fighting arm'.

Those who care about Palestine ask in bewilderment why, if Muslims are good people, why are they being killed in Gaza? Why are they being starved to death? What crime have they done to deserve this?' Such questions come from an ill-informed, unreal world, of fantasy, of science-fiction. It is very sad. These people do not ask what have the people of Iraq done, or what have the people of Uganda, Angola, Sudan, Cambodia, Bangladesh, Burma, Nepal, Tibet, Indonesia, Nigeria, India, Pakistan, Afghanistan, Zimbabwe, El Salvador, Nicaragua, Bosnia Herzegovina, etc, etc, etc, etc, done. Are the people of those countries also not good people? Why do they have to suffer, to be displaced, homeless and starving?

One day, the human race will wake up to the realities of our world and join together to help change it. Even killing all the leaders in the Israeli Government - or of any Government for that matter - will not make the slightest difference to the way things are, as the new leaders, even if they come from a totally different political party, will be the same, will do the same.

Politicians do not run the world. The world is run by those who make money out of politicians. Banks, Media Moguls, the top military, Defence Ministers, Churches, weapon manufacturers. They dictate the fate of peoples, of countries, not the politicians, who 'pretend' they run the world. Until we understand this truth and take action to change the system we live in, and finish with a militarised world, all our ranting, all the Peace demonstrations, are useless for achieving Peace. On the contrary, we simply help justify more violence.

Peace Forums often come to the conclusion that what we need to do is try together to come up with a workable plan at peace and reconciliation, to see if it can be done in a way that will be both fair and reasonable to both sides, taking into consideration the cultural, political, and physical needs and aspirations of both sides. Yes. But first we have to understand precisely why we are in this mess. It seems to me that most people believe that politicians do not know what to do, and there is war after war in many corners of the world, because no Civil Peace Group or NGO has come up to politicians with a good plan! We have war after war because this is not so. Politicians make conflict happen.

We need to understand why we have wars and finish with a militarised world. If we did, we would soon realize that politicians, like all diplomats, are salesmen who are paid to say one thing but to do something else. They have to pretend they are working for Peace, maybe even believing their own stance, when in reality, they are not doing anything other than saying what they are told and paid to say.

The elites who protect politicians expect them to take into consideration the cultural, political and physical needs and aspirations of all sides, but this, only makes the creation of conflict, of war, easier. One side knows very well what will enrage the other, so this is what they have to do. I will repeat it endlessly: politicians have no control; Banks, weapon manufacturers, Media barons, Churches, oil, land and gold barons do. Through diplomats and secret services, Governments are fed with information - false most of the time - that will lead to war. Governments use that false information to brainwash the credulous masses.

Any Peace proposal must start with the education of the masses, explaining to them 'why' they suffer, why they have to suffer, who benefits from their suffering and why politicians cannot be blamed entirely. They are easily manipulated, not because they are meek or unintelligent. It is their greed - for money and power - that betrays them.

The same applies to the Police in many countries. You can be a regular policeman all your working life, but any aspirations to the top job, means that you have to reach one of the high echelons of Freemasonry in Britain. In some countries, the 'ruling elite' could be the Military, in others, the Church, in others, oil barons. How do you reach this high degree? You must prove you are a blind and obedient member.

So, a policeman reaches the top position, earns a huge salary, becomes famous, ego boosted to high levels. He, and it is always he, gains respect from society, and so on. But - and this is the big 'But' - the reality is, a person with a double life is born. To society, he has to show how much effort he is making to protect the population from crime, to decrease or even eradicate crime. He must show how much he is against prostitution and drugs, show how he protects democracy by allowing street demonstrations, gay rights, and so on.

However, in reality, his real duties are to **protect** certain prostitutes, arrest 'private' drug dealers, because they are competition to the Government dealers who tour the country. And he has to cooperate with the secret services, to **promote** strikes, civil revolts, riots, terrorism and crimes.

Society has a lot of work to do, a lot of thinking, if it really wants to change and improve our world.

Dear Ahed,

If you really feel that much better through your belief in God, I am not going to argue with you. However, I hope you can answer my questions. You wrote:

'..... to satisfy the sick minded brutal regimes in Palestine/Israel.' Whilst I agree with you about those 'sick minded' people, do not you know that many of them have been 'forced' to act as if sick minded? In fact, they become 'really' sick afterwards. I know hundreds of soldiers in continuous medical treatment or in psychotherapy, because of the crimes they have committed, against their will.

Furthermore, don't you yet know that these unfortunate fighters are not acting to satisfy themselves? The only satisfied people are the weapon manufacturers and all the intermediary traders. This includes Bankers, politicians, and oil and press barons. You speak of 'those innocents from both sides', but don't you know that this is precisely why we keep having wars? There are so many innocent people. To politicians and warmongers, innocence is the same as ignorance, which in turn means 'easy to brainwash'.

You ask that GOD 'guide their families to overcome these tragedies, and accept all victims in your heaven'. Can you explain to me, dear Ahed, if God is so good and powerful, couldn't he have avoided all those untimely deaths in the first place? It shouldn't be too difficult for God to make those machine guns or bombs become ineffective.

Now, assuming God was having a nap when the tragedies occurred and woke up too late, in which 'heaven' will he receive them? You speak of 'your heaven', in singular. Do you mean there is only one heaven? If that is the case, why did God create so many religions? What's the point in separating humanity here on Earth, if they'll all end up living eternally together in Heaven?

Ahed, answer my questions, please !!!!

Thank you.

Alberto

25

NOTES TO A PALESTINIAN JOURNALIST

It is all very obvious to me, that your suffering has darkened your vision, both from the physical as well as from the intellectual point of view.

If you think that tiny Israel, founded 60 years ago, with 4 million people, can control one of the largest countries in the world - the USA - independent since 1776, with 200 million people - you are very confused. Where did you get this idea from? You are worsening the situation of your people and of the world with such an incorrect, untrue idea.

The US decided on 'Full Spectrum Dominance' before Israel existed and, because of the stupidity or the willingness not to interfere with America's sinister plan of politicians the world over, the US is achieving this.

When I was a child, America had 70 military bases outside the US. They now have several hundred, half of them nuclear.

Your continuous defence of what you call 'rational' murderers - Hitler, Sharon, suicide bombers - demonstrate that you do not really want Peace and do not really respect all human life. You justify all kind of atrocities, as long as it can be 'proved' to your satisfaction that they are 'logical' atrocities.

I urge you to revise your view of the world, please! Do not tell us again something just because other people believe it or because books have been written about it. **You** are the journalist. If you want to be a really **good** journalist, you must find the truth for yourself and not allow yourself to be influenced by other people's agendas.

You are still confusing Nationality with ethnicity. Please, do not continue to make the same mistake as most people. You talk about a conflict between Arabs and Israelis. Arabs are an ethnic group and Israelis are those born in Israel or immigrants from any country in the world who adopted Israeli nationality. In fact, many Arabs are Israeli. You also have British Arabs, Brazilian Arabs, and so on.

The problem is between Israelis and Palestinians because you are disputing a piece of land, not ethnicity. In fact, both groups, Israelis of Middle-Eastern origin and Palestinians, are all the same ethnic group. The fact that some of you practice the Muslim religion and others the Jewish religion, does not give you different ethnicity.

I once amused myself studying the attire of five Jewish men. One of them was from Israel, two from Turkey and two from Yemen. All dressed in traditional Arab gear. I then looked at five Muslims – one from Saudi Arabia, one from Lebanon, two Israelis and one Egyptian, all wearing Western style suits. Not even a fanatic Jew or fanatic Muslim could tell who was what.

Ethnicity is determined by the country you are born in, or your parents' country of origin. For instance, two Iraqis, one Muslim, the other Jewish or Christian look the same. Two Ethiopians of different religions will also look alike. However, take two Muslims, one from Iraq, the other from Ethiopia - and they look very different. A Catholic from Italy will look very different to a Catholic from Bolivia or Nigeria. But take two Nigerians, one Muslim and the other Catholic, and they look the same. As humans devoid of race or ethnicity, or indeed, nationality, we are all the same.

You say of suicide bombers: 'They think that this is the only choice left for them. Either defeat and humiliation... or death this way'. You also say that their behaviour is rational. Does that make you an 'irrational' person, because you do not go and blow yourself up with a bomb in your pocket or tied around your waist?

You know very well that violence engenders violence. So, the rationale of accepting a violent act, means by default that you agree with more, never ending violence.

You say of Israel that 'They have at their disposal the world's second most powerful army,' ignoring that Russia, England and China come before them in the sordid list of powerful, large armies.

'They (Israel) have America at their beck and call,' you say. But, America is at the beck and call of any country that is willing to use their weapons to enrich the coffers of the USA treasury.

Look how many American weapons there are in the Philippines, because this country not only buys American weapons but also gives plenty of space to America, for them to have military bases with thousands of soldiers occupying them.

And you then say, 'there is, of course, the impotent and international community which has failed to give Palestinians justice.' They are trying my friend. Believe me, they are trying, but it takes time for the international community to forget all of the French, Belgian, Italians, Germans, Japanese, Americans, - military and civilian - that have died not only in Israel but in many European countries from PLO bombs, grenades, landmines and machine gun attacks.

I told you before, violence engenders violence. It is not fair that you want the whole world to know only of the atrocities committed by Israel on Palestinians. It is also not fair that you want the whole world, which includes the families of many who died (not only Jews, but Muslims, Catholics, Protestants, and other faiths) because of Palestinian activities, to forgive and forget.

In addition, we have (as I always say and will not tire of saying) scientists working on weapon research, the weapon manufacturers, weapon traders and Governments, who are doing everything they can to make sure the conflict never stops. Unless countries unite in saying, 'Basta !!! Enough is enough!!!' and demand an international law that forces all Governments on Earth to get rid of their Armed Forces by never buying another weapon and destroying all the weapons they have.

There will never be Peace, Justice and Human Rights, unless we close all the manufacturing plants of guns, tanks, grenades, landmines, bombs, air-fighters, warships, military submarines, the entire hardware of war. I say again, unless we stop the War business, there will never be Peace. This will initially create lots of bankruptcies and mass unemployment, but Governments should then bail out all factories who change their range of product from items causing death to those that will prolong life. Equally, with scientists. Money should go 'exclusively' to scientists developing new medicinal drugs or treatments for improving the health of people, not into projects for destroying it.

Who brainwashed you? How can you believe that F-16 fighters and other state-of-the-art machines of death were designed to be used against powerful 'armies' only? If that were the case, the 'war industry' would be in a total state of collapse!

You speak about F-16, as if the air-fighter itself was a weapon. This is bizarre: the aircraft is not a weapon. It could also be used for reaching places in a short time – though because of the high speeds they can reach, they cannot go very far. F-16s are not made for long travelling. They are made for reaching heights at great speeds, to drop bombs (also at great speed) and return to base. They are to bombs what guns and rifles are to bullets.

What I am trying to say is that F-16s and all other air-fighters are made for killing and destroying property. Once we allow their construction, we should not complain about their use. If we do not want buildings and lives destroyed, we should oppose productions of air-fighters and warships.

The 'weapon' is the bomb carried. Bombs are not made to distinguish between a 'powerful Army' and a 'family sleeping'. Bombs are for killing, killing and killing, for destroying buildings, bridges, factories or anything hit by them.

As you do not campaign against bombs, (and other missiles) your protest against their use is meaningless to me. Your rantings against Nazi-Jews, Nazi-Israel, become worthless. The same bombs the Israeli Armed Forces use are bought and used by Muslims in Pakistan and elsewhere. Why do not you write about the Nazi-Muslim Army of Pakistan, using Nazi techniques to decimate the Hindu population?

To bomb manufacturers, the 'style' of their clients, whether they have a Nazi mind, Fascist mind, capitalist, communist, does not matter in the least. No questions are asked of anybody who comes with the money to buy bombs.

I have nothing more to say. If to you, Muslims never kill, and only Jews, Hindus and Christians practice the 'Art of Killing', it means that you consciously wish to ignore the history of Islam.

Since you do not seem interested in history, perhaps you should obtain reports on weapon contracts from CAAT (Campaign Against Arms Trade). The biggest and main clients of weapon manufacturers are Muslim. Come to London to the International Arms Fair and see for yourself the prospective clients looking at the exhibits. A large percentage of them are Arabs.

Without the Muslim trade, the weapon world would be in a dire state. I hope you understand me - I am not defending or saying anything conciliatory about Christians, Jews or Hindus. We are all the same. To weapon manufacturers, the religion of the buyer does not matter. What matters is that the buyer has the money to buy; whether they arrange their own or use Banks and other financial institutions that act as 'brokers' of the deal.

Why do you waste so much time discussing things that lead nowhere? Do you read what goes on in the world? Do you know what happened a few years ago in Haiti? The US, Britain, France, Israel, having armed -and sold many arms -to create a rebel army, prepared the country for a Civil War. Weapon manufacturers and politicians then sat in their comfortable armchairs in front of big television screens, to watch the fireworks. The US is now sending marines to Haiti. They must be kept busy - and it also helps the weapons industry. Wars also give countries a good excuse to raise taxes.

My friend, whilst you do not see how Israel and Palestine are only two pieces of the game of political chess played by the powers, a game also known as 'war', there will never be peace in the Middle East. Do not accept my words because I utter them. I urge you to be sceptical, to read - AND ANALYSE - the world news, history, the speeches of politicians and how so many of them constantly lie.

I heard an Ambassador to Qatar say everything a Muslim -and sometimes anti-Jew- wanted to hear. A few years later, the same Ambassador was in Israel. I heard him say only what Israeli Jews wanted to hear. This is the world of Politics, of diplomacy. The world of lies. I am not saying that it is easy to say the truth, only that you should NEVER take what you hear and see the way politicians want you to. You should analyse, analyse and analyse. And then, you should interpret. It is what we musicians do in music. The printed score means absolutely nothing. It is a succession of black stains on a piece of white paper. That is NOT the music. The music is what you do not see. The composer's message cannot be written. Your suffering, the suffering for your people, makes you not see clearly what is really happening and what has been going on since 1948.

'Indeed all Israeli occupying forces and all settlers deserve as much pain,' you say. You **totally** forget that wishing, 'only' wishing, the suffering of others, is a moral sin and something that can only bring more suffering upon you and your people. The Mystic Law clearly explains 'Cause and Effect'. Not only it is wrong to kill somebody, it is also wrong to only 'wish' his death.

You continue, 'They – the settlers - are the reasons for the Palestinian suffering, they are the main reason for the Middle East crisis'. You again **completely** forget that 95% of the settlers and the occupying forces are there against their will and the 5% that are 'for' it, is only because they have been brain-washed by the propaganda and 'material benefits' to be 'for'.

As for 'the Middle-East crisis', you do not seem interested in international politics and are not aware of the moves by powerful governments.

If Israel did not exist, world powers would find other means to create a troubled Middle East. The long years of suffering of the Lebanese people, the devastating conflicts in Cyprus, the Iran-Iraq war, the Iraqi invasion of Kuwait - and subsequent conflict with NATO forces - the Turkish, Iranian and Iraqi massacre of the Kurdish people - the list is unending - would have all happened even if Israel did not exist.

You rightly say, '...Islam favours strength to face the enemy' Well my friend, you should know - that in order to prove your strength against an enemy, you need to create an enemy first. This is what Christianity, Islam and Judaism do, create enemies, so that they can prove their strength. They also do it within the divisions existing in same religion. Think of the Iran-Iraq war or the Civil Wars in Ireland and Spain.

When a football game takes place, the losing team suffers and the winning team celebrates their win as well as the suffering of the losing team. Religions and the Military, who go 'hand-in-hand', also need this 'suffering of the losers' in order to feel strong. With your attitude, you are converting life into a game of 'winners and losers' and this will NEVER help the situation.

Whilst you do not teach everybody – and by everybody I mean people of all religions and nationalities - that we are ALL equal, that the Earth belongs to all of us, that we all have the same rights, you will not help the cause of Peace.

I have Christian friends who, in some Muslim countries, could not buy a house because only Muslims can do that. Even their work permits there have been extended with enormous difficulties and only after paying a lot of money to certain officials. It is nothing against my friends personally, but religions always take steps towards the creation of inter-religion tensions and enemies.

In Israel, it is the same. Jewish Estate Agents with some Muslim friends are often in the difficult situation of having to deny, under Government instructions, the purchase of houses in certain areas, by these Muslim friends. All this does is create enemies. This is what religions do: create separation and division.

Militaries are the same. Take the recent death of the Macedonian President, who genuinely wanted to stop the war in his country, a war promoted by NATO. He infuriated NATO and their allies the military industry. So, when flying over a NATO air-controlled zone, his plane was made to crash.

You are a journalist. You are in a position to educate your readership. Open the mind of the reader. Governments and religions brainwash. You should make your readers think, otherwise we carry on in this vicious circle, and nothing will ever change.

Read, Please, Read carefully, and try to understand how violence and hatred between humans is promoted all the time by those in power.

I am asking you to 'know' how the world works and to pass on your knowledge to your readers.

In Peace.

Dear Ahed

The vast majority of people all over the world want to live in peace. Palestinian, Israeli, Angolan, Sudanese, Pakistani Iraqi people from all countries WANT Peace. With illness, accidents and natural events like floods, earthquakes, fires, hurricanes we already have enough human suffering.

Sadly, the people who run the world are not interested in what the majority of people want. Why do you think Israeli newspapers – despite anti government articles by Uri Avneri, Gideon Levy, Amira Hess and the like - keep publishing anti-Palestinian thoughts and Palestinian publications write anti-Israeli articles? Why don't newspapers on both sides fill the pages with articles and photographs of all the villages where Jews and Muslims live together as one family? Such stories could fill entire newspapers! If you believe that Israelis and Palestinians cannot live together, happily and in Peace, you also are the victim of brain washing that Press Barons, in conspiracy with Governments, are happy to promote. And I say Press Barons because so many journalists would like to promote Peace but should they dare to publish their own opinions, they would be looking for a new job the next day.

Thousands of years ago, before agriculture was 'invented' or discovered, man depended for his survival on whatever he could find in nature. So, if there was a shortage of food, he had neighbours he could turn to in order to feed his family or group. This is no longer the case. In our modern world, there is enough food for everyone. If, for whatever reason – a flood or a drought - we cannot grow food to eat – there are plenty of ways for those with a surplus of food to help. As for invading territory, we know the size of the planet and know that there is room for everyone. Eliminate militarism, educate humans into learning how to live as humans - all as one family - and we can leave a better place for the world's children. For our children and grandchildren. Believe me, It can be done!

Alberto

26

BUREAUCRACIES, FEAR AND STRONG OPINION

What stands in the way of a negotiated Peace in the Israel/Palestine conflict when polls show that over 60% of Israelis and of Palestinians favour it? Could the blame lie with fear or the bureaucracies in charge? To me - and the amount of people I speak to is 'almost' like a poll! - more than 60%, possibly 80%, favour a negotiated peace. But, even if 95% of Palestinians and Israelis favoured such negotiation, it would still not be put in place. Peace, like war, does not happen because a majority of the population wants it. It happens because the small minority, who run the world, wants it.

This is how it has been throughout history. Napoleon did not ask the French people if they wanted him to invade Croatia or Russia. The Catholics Kings of Spain did not ask the Spanish population if they wanted all Jews dead - or equally when to stop killing Jews.

Hitler did not produce the Holocaust because 60% of German inhabitants 'favoured' the slaughter. Nobody asked the Iraqi population if they wanted their country invaded and destroyed. No need to go any further. We have many thousands of examples, throughout history, that those who run the world are not influenced by what people think and want.

When we speak of 'fear', whom do populations fear? What is this 'fear'? It must be the fear **people** have, because politicians and warmongers, merchants of death, have no fear. It is important to be aware of how 'fear' is a planned, very carefully planned feeling, created by Governments, with the help of psychologists and experts in mind and mass control and the assistance of the Media.

So, does blame lie with the 'bureaucracies in charge'? Speaking of the 'bureaucracies in charge' gives the impression that politicians are in charge, but they are not. Those 'in charge' are the people whom politicians obey. If they do not, they must 'go', like Lincoln and Kennedy, to give you just two examples. Those men - and women – 'in charge' are influential bankers, industrialists, oil and gold barons, Churches, Vatican, royal families, and/or freemasons. Most of them belonging to the Bilderberg Group or other such groups.

How many bureaucracies have changed in 60 years in Israel and Palestine? And what difference did it make? Bureaucracies are only a screen, so that populations do not to see who is really running the world.

Why do you think 'Peace' negotiations are always held in secret? Why are not even political analysts or journalists allowed in? In these meetings, politicians discuss when to have wars and how big or long the war should be. Once a war has started, cabinets meet. They study the financial circumstances, military strategies, how many bombs they have got left, how much longer they can go on fighting and which countries to invade next.

At the end of 'negotiations', they then open the doors to the waiting journalists and come up with the great news that they have been discussing Peace and that Peace is imminent. If, at the meeting they decided to attack each other, they say to journalists that negotiations have failed. This is not my 'opinion'. It is my 'experience'.

Khomeini went back to Iran from his exiled domicile in France, thanks to Washington and the CIA. On one occasion, the CIA paid several million dollars for religious leaders and their rogue assistants, to organize a one million crowd demonstration in Teheran. One million people - 98% of them very poor - suddenly had the means of travelling huge distances to descend upon the Iranian capital, with money to pay for travel, hotels and food.

I've seen this all of my life. Every time Washington decided the Government of my beloved Argentina (or other Latin American countries) should go, that was it. The CIA, with the assistance of the local US Embassy, and with US taxpayers money, infiltrated all unions, syndicates, Universities - and ..... that was it! General, national strikes, mass demonstrations, inflation, bomb explosions and ...suddenly, a military coup. Thus another few years of military dictatorship. Of course, countries have the choice, like Poland right now – to give big chunks of land to Washington, to install yet more US military bases. This has been the history of the world, for the last 150 years.

As to the reasons for invading Iraq, Bush and the Democrats (particularly with the Clinton couple) are great friends and partners. Clear proof is in the invitation Bill Clinton received from Bush Senior and Reagan, to succeed them in the White House. The first of Bill Clinton's election campaigns was financed and masterminded accordingly. The Republican chiefs were very grateful to Clinton for allowing – when he was Governor of Arkansas, to have all the drugs imported from Colombia discreetly, landing at the Mena airstrip in airplanes belonging to the DEA (Drug Enforcement Agency). For once, the US Government had not been very subtle, as the DEA does precisely what it says - usually names mean the opposite of what they really stand for. The DEA makes sure drugs are 'enforced' on the population.

Of course, when carriers flew in the opposite direction, they were full of US made weapons. Bush could not care less about the Republican Party. He has exploited them and squeezed out as much juice - and blood -as he could from them. He is only interested in himself, that is: his oil interests. This is why, when the US invaded Iraq, he said, 'This is going to be a long affair'. He knew what he was saying, because he knew his personal plans. How many American and other soldiers, or how many Iraqi citizens or international journalists died in the process of his becoming richer, did not matter to him.

And it still does not matter, despite him not playing golf any more! So, if in Iran more people die, this is 'good for business', for Bush, for his partners in the oil business and for his close friends, the weapon manufacturers. Once he creates the mess, 'Hilarious' Clinton, Barack Obama, or whoever runs the Government, will take over the mess.

When it is said that Ahmadinijad is the real enemy of Iran and Islam, I smile. He, like Bush, is neither friend nor foe of anybody. He's interested in himself. He says and does things that benefit his personal Bank account and that of several members of his Cabinet. If his intention were to destroy Israel then he would not reveal it, even if it were not true. What matters, according to what psychologists specializing in mass control tell Governments to do, is to create fear and tension. Without it, the Arms Trade and a militarised world cannot prosper.

In fact, when Saddam invaded Kuwait, in August 1990, that was also arranged 'via' the CIA. This allowed US intervention, via NATO. These US strategies are history. It was so obvious the way they did it in World War II, when Prescott Bush, Ford and all the US illuminati financed and helped - with all kinds of advice - Adolf Hitler.

I always feel surprised that people condemn the violence, but not the weapons that produce that violence. People say many times that they do not like rockets, do not like bombs. In the same vein, we despair because 'people will die', or at Ahmadinejad's madness. But we are all so close to the REAL 'MAD' people, and we say nothing about them. Just consider the US, a country that has a military budget from which half a million scientists dedicated to destroy humanity receive their salary.

So many Universities from East to West and North to South of the United States have contracts with CIA, FBI and the US Armed Forces and what they invent must be tested and sold. You cannot test a bomb in space. You need to drop it and see the effect for real. This is how different manufactures can compete against each other.

Already, 60 years ago, the US 'had to test' the atomic bomb and chose Japan for the experiment.

I frankly cannot understand how we go on and on, accusing the poor military that follow orders, many of them traumatised for life, for what they are doing. Or we criticise politicians, who take orders from their 'paymasters': the weapon industrialists, Banks and oil barons.

If Ahmadinejad is mad, it is quite understandable. I bet that if any one of us were, at this moment in time, the President or Prime Minister of Iran, we would also go mad! And if we 'refused' to go mad, that is, if we never bought and used a Russian missile or tried to establish good relations with Israel, the CIA would get rid of us.

In the US, as in Britain, most of the Universities that teach Peace Studies have the most active science departments dedicated to promote wars. One of the most famous such Universities is MIT, in Boston. Have a look at the MIT website and you'll have a taste of the wars to come.

You may say that these are strong opinions. When I am criticised for expressing 'strong' opinions, I understand what people mean. What I want to stress is that even when expressing my opinions strongly and with conviction, I am aware that I could be wrong. In fact, I often wish that I were wrong.

Dear Ahed,

Thank you very much for trusting my judgement, although, as always, I say, 'I wish I were wrong'.

You say, 'I do believe that Ahmadinijad is the real enemy of Iran and Islam'. But he, like Bush, is neither friend nor foe of anybody. He's interested in himself. He says and does things that benefit his personal Bank account and that of several members of his Cabinet.

You say, 'If his intention is destroying Israel then why to reveal that?' I am sure you understand that he MUST reveal it, even if it is not true. What matters, according to what psychologists specializing in mass control tell Governments to do, is to create fear and tension. Without it, the Arms Trade and a militarised world cannot prosper.

In fact, when Saddam invaded Kuwait, 18 years ago, it was also arranged 'via' CIA, to allow for US intervention. These US strategies are history. It was so obvious the way they did it in World War II, when Prescott Bush, Henry Ford and all the US illuminati – including the Federal Reserve and the 'Vatican Bank' - financed Adolf Hilter, and helped, with all kind of advice. Hitler or no Hitler, Jews or no Jews, Holocaust or no Holocaust, World War II had to happen. It was in the agenda of the oligarchs who run the world.

Alberto

27
EDUCATION

As a child and since childhood, I have been very puzzled as to why little children had to be taught to sing patriotic songs, recognize military marches and know to whom they were dedicated, which hero was being lauded. I was intrigued when I learnt that those 'heroes' were all people who had become part of our history because they had killed more than others. More of a mystery was to know that many of these famous men had been paid to organize military campaigns and slaughter.

In other words, as a child, I was quite confused. On one hand I knew that people who committed murder were sent to prison, but other murderers were paid by Governments to do the same thing and were applauded for it. Strange world, I used to think!

During my secondary education, I understood that invading

countries with mercenary armies was an expensive practice, which led me to realize why countries had imposed compulsory military service. Big armies at very low cost.

This practice, I thought, had been learnt from the Churches, who always had their own armies, with the difference that previously soldiers had been told they had to kill to defend God. What irony, as all defended the same God, the creator of the world, and now they were told they had to kill to defend their country.

The Arms Trade has given Governments such boost or stimulus, that many countries around the Globe decided there is no need for compulsory armies. So, they train and pay professionals. Globalisation has had a certain effect on patriotism and religion and not as many people as would be desired join branches of the Armed Forces. The solution was found in educating people to become young men and women attracted by guns, bombs, torture, and war. In other words, by attracting them to violence. By making them violent. The teaching of patriotism and of religious bigotry continues to this day, as Churches and politicians need religious fanatics and patriots to carry out their murderous plans - plans that would not exist if weapons did not exist. Or, more accurately, if the Arms Trade did not exist.

As I said before, the teaching of patriotism and of religious bigotry continues to this day. In the same way that temples belonging to different religions will decorate their walls, and practitioners will decorate the walls of their homes, with items belonging to the religion they practice, the same do Governments. They litter the country - via parks, squares, public buildings - with portraits and statues of criminals (I call 'criminal' what Governments call 'hero'). They want to remind the world of how many people these 'brave patriots' killed. They want children to grow thinking 'the best way to be remembered after death, to be famous, is by becoming a military and win wars'.

The Ministry of Education, in any country of the world, does not work for Peace. They work to support Government's aims through 'education'.

This means, if a country wishes to have wars, the Ministry of Education has to devise educational methods that will produce young people willing to fight, kill and be killed.

Take the Ministry of Education in North Korea. They have to produce, under CIA instructions, an anti-US population to maintain tensions. So, what exercises did the Ministry devise to teach children how to divide 30 by 3? This is the exercise: 30 American enemy soldiers have been shot dead by North Korean soldiers. Each Korean soldier killed an equal number of enemy soldiers. How many enemy soldiers did each North Korean soldier kill?

This is 'Official Education' for you! Of course, these politicians (actors, diplomats, professional liars) have to pretend they are working for Peace. Some of them are such good actors, that they really make populations believe they are working for Peace. The paradox is that they may well be very interested in Peace, but they are not working for the people, even less for Peace-seekers; they are working for those above them, who control them. An elite that ' feeds' on wars, injustice and human suffering. Politicians are only a temporary 'instrument' in the plan of the elites who run the world and for whom they work. The efforts MUST come from us to oppose Ministry of Education's 'education'.

I am a realist. When I say politicians are oblivious to the past, to history, I mean, for instance, the decades, since the creation of the Jewish State of Israel, of group after group, Jews and Muslims, Israeli and Palestinian, practicing all those joint activities, teaching respect and love of each other.

However, if after teaching human love, you need politician to sign a Peace Treaty, it only means, all the work was in vain. I am an optimist, but I have, over a period of about 40 years, proved that I speak the truth, the unpalatable truth.

Very interestingly, in Britain, where the number of young people recruited by the Armed Forces has declined and when an increasingly cosmopolitan population could make this decline more dramatic, Government has come up with the solution. As I write these pages, on Sunday 23 March 2008, I read in the front page of The Sunday Times 'Britons free at last to fly the flag'. The first sentence of the article reads 'Public buildings, including job centres, schools and hospitals, are to be encouraged to fly the union jack and other national flags, to boost national identity'.

This means only one thing: that Government is planning new conflicts, new wars. Making patriots, making children grow up feeling they must be prepared to 'give their life for their country', is the first step to a commitment to violence and war.

Of course in countries where there still is compulsory military service, young men and women have no option. They must kill and be killed just because the Authority says so, but in countries where entering the military is a career or occupation like becoming a teacher, plumber, lorry driver, car mechanic, musician, doctor, etc., you need to create a Youth who is 'weapon-loving', 'violence-worshippers and practitioners'.

This is achieved through education. Religion and history at school, and cinema, television and games, outside school. Religion and history teach you how our ancestors 'solved all their problems' through war. Not one religion or history teacher dares say, 'They could have dialogued instead of killing each other'. All battles are given as examples of 'how great our men were'.

Educating young people into a love of violence, weapons, bombs, killing, is very easy and does not need very intelligent or well prepared teachers, but brain-washing young people into feeling patriotic, dreaming of becoming heroes, takes a bit of an effort. So here, trained educationalists and psychologists are used, not only to prepare young people to become professional murderers, but also to make them happy about the prospect of coming back home a corpse. The special 'training' also involves the immediate family of the innocent victim, to brainwash them into proclaiming - when they see the unfortunate corpse - that their son, brother, husband, died a 'hero'.

With this human ignorance - or as Hitler called it - stupidity, politicians are happy in the knowledge they can continue to make money. As long as they can stay put in their offices, together with weapon manufacturers, Bankers, Church leaders, press, oil and gold barons, and innocent 'patriots' are prepared to go and kill and be killed on their behalf, they are happy.

Public 'education' frequently occurs through the press. Since I mentioned Press barons, it is important to stress the role they play in the game of war. They are real conspirators. I just give one example, but the same happens the world over. In Iraq, on 2 April 2008, the press reported that in March, almost a thousand people died and several thousands were wounded, as a result of fighting between Iraqi security forces and Shia militiamen.

However, no newspaper or no journalist, including those who write editorials or opinions, will ask the question: how can the militiamen be so well armed? Who provides them with arms? Who buys them for them? How do the weapons reach their hands? They do not approach the subject, because they are all accomplices or partners in the game. The game of fighting. Governments, foreign as well as the same Iraqi authorities, make sure the militiamen are equipped for fighting.

It is the same in Colombia. The FARC fighters receive their endless supply of weapons from the same US authorities that supply the Colombian Government. How many people die in Colombia it is not an US problem. The US only wants the Colombian drugs and for them to use US made weapons.

The error lies always in the fact that people believe the US is going to help them, when the reality is that if an American diplomat does something against the financial interests of Washington, he'll loose his job, or be assassinated. Of course the same happens with British diplomats and those from all countries. Their mission is always to look after the interests of the country they represent.

Ahed,

As several times before, I say to you, you are proof of enlightment!!!! Your writing in response to Laura's comments is accurate, fair and above all, considering the life of exile in various countries you have had, very objective.

I agree that aggressive words should not be used in this Peace Forum. As to Khalid's support of Hamas, what can I do? I let him have his opinion. I would not support Hamas and I think nobody should support Hamas, but on the other hand, I know that, the way our economical and financial system works, if Hamas disappeared tomorrow, the Governments of Israel, Palestine and the US, with the assistance of their secret agents, would simply create another such movement.

Alberto

28

A CONVERSATION WITH KHALID AMAYREH
Palestinian journalist and author.

A. If you want to believe Mohammed was illiterate, that is your choice. With the studies he did and the life he led, there is no way I will ever believe that. Besides, Mohammed's most important wife, who allowed him to have the Army he wanted, had plenty of time to complete his education. An illiterate man could NOT organise and train an army, then plan and carry out attacks with the details and strategies used by Mohammed. Also, in his life, he had contact with scientists of his time, learnt a lot, and, as the intelligent man he was, he deduced things.

K. Alberto, I do not think that your remarks reflect a person who is well informed in matters of religion and philosophy and metaphysics. As a Muslim, I believe that seas and mountains existed for millions of years. I also believe in the Nebula...how the world came into being. This is what the Quran says. These beliefs do not contradict my faith at all.

Most of these things are in the Quran. The Quran and Science are totally compatible. Believing in the Quran is not a blind faith. It is very much based on logic and science. For example, can you tell me how a man living in 6th century Arabia could master scientific facts that man only recently discovered? Can you tell me why there is not a single 'discrepancy' between the Quran and modern science? Ours is not a blind faith. I am not an uneducated person. And my views are at least as legitimate as yours'.

A. Of course! I respect your views. You misinterpret me fully. But, how could an illiterate man who appeared in Arabia 1500 years ago know scientific facts that scientists were able to discover only recently? Besides, the scientific 'facts' stated in the Quran were stated by Siddartha Gautama - Buddha – a thousand years earlier.

K. If you haven't read the Quran, I suggest you read it. Then you could be more qualified to argue with me.

A. I have read the Quran several times. Not for the sake of reading it, but as part of my religious studies and analysis. I discuss religion with imams, mullahs, priests and rabbis and not one of them has ever said to me 'you must read the Quran (or Bible) to be more qualified to argue with me'. You do not need to be a Muslim to believe the Quran. The difference between you and I is that you were told since you were born that a good Muslim does not question anything the Quran states. But I have always believed man is free to believe what he wants to believe, that is, I believe in 'freedom of thought', nobody is going to force me to believe something that does not convince me as truth. Since I do not believe in angels, (in the religious sense) I could never believe someone just appeared - on behalf of God - to speak to anybody. I have personally seen spirits all my life, since I was 9, so I know for sure this can happen, but spirits never said they were sent by God.

K. What is your definition of 'spirit.'?

A. Spirit is the force of life that animates the body of living things.

K. Do you believe in the existence of non-material beings?

A. Yes. When the material body dies, the spirit does not die. For the spirit to live by itself, the body must die first

K. If you believe in spirits, you believe in non-material beings. It means there is a metaphysical world. And, if you do, how come you do not believe in God? You contradict yourself, in other words

A. Believing in spirits is one thing, but believing that one of those spirits came first, to create us, is something totally different. If you really believe everything must have a creator, then who created God? How could someone who did not exist, decide he wanted to exist?

God (Allah) was never a human being, so I cannot see how he could become a spirit, unless he is the spirit of a dinosaur or some other remote creature that lived in our planet before humans started to appear.

I believe in Forces of the Universe, Forces of Nature, who are there, have 'always' been there. To me the Universe is infinite, has no beginning and no end, and there is continuous transformation.

It is a very long subject and one that I cannot at this time of night, and very tired, continue to develop; however, I hope I have said enough to clarify my thinking.

Christians have always used the same strategy. Every time they want donations (a lot of money), they find a poor woman, ignorant, illiterate, to say that an angel, or the Virgin Mary, appeared to her. A Bishop from Rome is then sent to confirm the story and consecrate the place and a new moneymaking venture is born. Mohammed was very ambitious and he learned the ruse from Christians. People who worshipped the moon, the sun, did not have to give money or their life. But, once you put God into your business plan, that's it - it never fails.

In fact, had everybody in the Middle East - Mesopotamia been a devout Christians, enriching the coffers of the Vatican, Islam would have never been born. There are several historians who analyse how it was the Vatican's idea to create a movement that would make so many pagans believe in God. The original idea was to use this group and once they converted atheists into God-worshippers, they'd unite to become even more powerful than they already were.

Little did they imagine the religion they encouraged, Islam, was going to become their worst enemy. It is this rivalry that has resulted in endless wars, which continue to this day and will continue for as long as religions exist.

In the Quran, verses that instruct Islam to 'invade Spain' DO NOT EXIST. This is my point. Religion is only used for men to do what they want. Power, power and power, is all they seek. Only if they said the truth - 'we want to become a bigger country, a richer country, the most powerful human group in the world' - they would get nowhere. Nobody would support them. However, tell your soldiers the battle is in the name of God and you can go ahead, invading countries, murdering millions.

K. No, No, Islam would never say, 'you have to accept…..it is truth.'!!! Islam says 'think, think, and think' Islam says, *'Innama Yakhsa ALlaha min Ibadihi al Ulmaa.'* 'Only the truly knowledgeable will be conscious of their Lord.' All or most of your information about the Muslim world is fictitious….out of touch with reality. It seems you have a reality of your own.

A. If I have a reality of my own, you have the fantasy of the many. According to Islam, the 'truly knowledgeable' are those who recite the Quran by heart, repeating every word like parrots, without ever trying to find out if what is written there is true or false.

Tell me what information I have that is fictitious. I'd like you to know that, apart from several translations by Muslims who speak and write English or French, I have specially quoted to you from the English translation by Marmaduke Pickthall, the Englishman who converted to Islam. This is - or was a few years ago - the translation approved for students of Islam at British Universities. Not only Islam but also none of the other theistic religions say that all the ills of the world come from God. It is true, some of them are the result of our misdeeds, but I would not say, as you do, that 'mostly' they are the result of our misdeeds.

For one person who dies in a car accident, because he had an overdose of alcohol in his blood while driving, you have 100 of innocent, even very religious people who die because they were hit by a car. If 30 innocent and wonderful human beings die, or lose their limbs, because someone put a bomb in the café they were in, where is the misdeed of these dead or maimed people? If you are born with a medical condition that you inherited from one of your parents, where is the misdeed you did in your mother's womb?

K. The right way is to move forward without impinging on truth, without falsifying history.

A. Believe me, dear friend, very few in this world are as truthful as I am. For not impinging on truth, I have risked my own life several times.

When religions became partly separate from states, politicians replaced religious bigotry with patriotic bigotry. It's all the same. As long as you get people to become either religious or patriotic, the mould is set. The rich and powerful are happy, because they know they'll remain in control of the masses.

K. I only engaged you in historical facts pertaining to Islam, the Quran and Muhammed, because the books of Sira (biography of the Prophet), and the vast bulk of Western Scholarship, agree on the basic things....which you do not accept - for example, that the Prophet was *Ummi*, illiterate.

A. This is not an argument at all. We are not arguing. We are only expressing opinions and feelings. I NEVER said you do not know about your religion. On the contrary, I know you know it extremely well. But I also know my friend, HOW you were brought up. So I know what you heard since you were born, apart from what you read and studied.

K Remember, I engaged you with regard to your disbelief in God, because this is a matter of faith and people should be free to decide for themselves.

A. Of course. In Argentina I grew up with very few Muslims around me (98% of the populations belonging to the Catholic Church), but, as someone interested in history and philosophy, I studied ALL religions. This is what initially led me to imams, rabbis and priests, as I had many questions for them and wanted answers.

K. I am not going to answer for priests and rabbis....or on behalf of Christians and Judaism, but...

A. In ALL cases, I ended up with the same answers, 'Alberto, you are right, but religion is faith. You have to accept what you are told as the truth.' 'The scriptures say the truth'. Some of them, priests, rabbis or imams, would go as far as to tell me that not believing in God was a sin and I was going to be punished.

I knew so many ultra-religious people who were in and out of hospital, lost limbs in accidents, an imam with lung cancer who died at a young age, I was NEVER going to accept this rubbish, that all these wonderful people were being 'punished' by god, for on the other hand I knew real bastards who were very happy, healthy and successful.

It did not take me long to realize that what happened to people on earth was NOT the decision of God, but the result of their own actions, or, in the case of illness, there often were hereditary elements and in the case of accidents, there was an element of luck, as well as of cause and effect. For instance, if a young man, who was not yet a very experienced driver, went too fast on the road and in a difficult or un-expected situation had an accident and lost his legs, I knew that it was just an accident. NO WAY any god-believing person was going to make me believe that there was some god in the sky who decided to punish the young man.

K. Islam does not say that all the ills of the world are from God...It is mostly as result of our misdeeds.

A. Imams, priests and rabbis have always said to me, 'Alberto, you are right'. And in London, I had a Moroccan friend who was the Head of a School of Islamic Studies. In London I also live within half a mile of two mosques, so I have plenty of opportunities to learn, to discuss the subject and to think.

I would like to add that for more than 20 years now, I have lost all my opportunities to work in Iraq, Syria, Pakistan and Indonesia, because those who invite me do so on condition that I will not reveal my beliefs. They fear I may influence those lambs that do not think. They NEED them all very religious, so that they are obedient and can be manipulated with ease. Religion is the best way of preventing a country in the Third World from developing. This way, it is easier for the authorities to continue organising wars and murder, whilst they become richer.

K. My aim is also to abolish armies and terminate violence. But one has to do it the right way without impinging on truth, without falsifying history.

A. You claim that your aim is also to abolish armies and terminate violence, but I have read you for years, not only in our Forum, but also in Al-Jazeera. I have NEVER read a word about your aim of abolishing armies. On the contrary, you have written on how un-just the war is between the mighty Israeli Army and their poor counterpart. You have often dreamt of a big Palestinian Army to properly fight Israel. Is this the right way for you? If that is the case, you should be happy with warmonger and death merchant Tony Blair, who is working hard on behalf of weapon manufacturers, to insure that Palestinians have access to many and sophisticated weapons, so that they can have a proper game of war with Israel. The Vatican is delighted with all this. Nothing could be better for them than Muslims and Jews killing each other. They are helping the Catholic corporation become even stronger.

I am surrounded by practicing Muslims and one very good friend of mine also chose The Quran for his Master's Thesis. Something that you do not seem to understand is that I do not argue with you. I respect all you say and I really admire you for having such staunch faith.

If I believe that neither the Quran nor the Bible are 100% accurate, it is my right to do so and you should not be upset by it. What I think is neither here nor there. It is just a thought.

All I am telling you is that, as I work for Peace in the world and hate militarism, I disapprove of religions that also create violence and suffering. Remember that politicians did not exist in the past. Churches and Governments were one and the same. Armies did not belong to a country; they belonged to Islam, Catholicism, Protestantism, Judaism, etc. People invaded and murdered each other in the name of their religion. Stupidly enough, all in the name of the SAME God.

The bigotry that creates so much violence and war is within the same religion. In Islam alone, take the bloody history of Egypt, look at the continued slaughter of Muslims by Muslims in Pakistan, Indonesia - there are so many examples. In Ireland, Christians versus Christians have been killing each other for centuries.

Of course, I know the ordinary religious person who practices his religion, is a very good person and I have nothing against him/her, but unfortunately, the 'heads' of each religion are not of the same thought. Their obligation is not to see that people have a better knowledge and understanding of religious writings. Their duty is to see that their religion becomes richer and more powerful.

To them, if this means wars, no problem, let's have wars! This is why religious corporations have always had such wonderful relationship with armies. Remember, my aim is to abolish armies and wars, not religions.

Here in England, some of the richest or more successful men have never finished school. Some of them own the biggest commercial empires, are multi-millionaires and still need people to write letters for them, because they can hardly read and their writing is full of spelling mistakes.

They are illiterate from the point of view that - like Mohammed - they never had any formal education, but - again like Mohammed - they are not illiterate in their minds, in their personalities. They are very clever, enlightened and ambitious people, who, through sheer effort and natural intelligence and flair, succeeded in life.

The difference is that all these businessmen are just happy to become powerful through money, are content with having a family, giving them a good and very luxurious life, like only millionaires can do and..... that's it. They do not have any ambitions of power over other men, control men, conquer lands, become part of the history of their country.

Mohammed too, he was such a type. Of course I do not condemn him; he had the right, like Napoleon and like many others, to be ambitious and domineering and I admire him for what he achieved in life.

However, this has nothing to do with our differences. I admire him for his military achievements and his charisma and you claim that none of this counts. For you, like for all religious people, he was an ordinary and ignorant man chosen by god and that god - perhaps too busy arranging cyclones, earthquakes and floods - couldn't be bothered to speak directly to Mohammed, so he sent his slave Gabriel to do the job.

This fantasy has resulted - and still results today - in SO MANY wars in the world. I shall denounce religion until my last day. Of course I denounce with the same conviction the fiction stories in all religions. Most people I know, who are prominent in their Church organisation, agree with me.

I tell you just one little story that happened to me at a party in Rome, attended by three Vatican priests who are friends of mine. In conversation I spoke about 'Virgin Mary' (the traditional way of calling Jesus' mother, as Catholicism claims she was a virgin who had the son of God). One of the priests said 'not virgin at all; if Joseph (her husband) is not Jesus' father, it means Mary had a lover'. Or she was raped, as Channel 4's Christmas TV Documentary in 2008 suggested.

Now, you say you're interested in true history. Unless you can bring back into existence all the documents that monarchs and religious leaders burnt up, so that they could distort history to their own advantage, you are never going to know the full truth of what really happened. Both religious and secular historians were not historians at all. They were people who could write. They were paid to write what was dictated to them by domineering leaders, political and religious authorities.

Remember, I work for Peace. Religions only bring wars. If you can't see it, or, if you do not mind all the injustice and suffering in the world, caused by religions, that is your decision. I do not argue and I do not wish to convince you of anything. Do continue with your beliefs, but I assure you, with 100% conviction, that religions are the poison of our world and the cause of 90% of human suffering.

I go back to your thinking on Mohamed. To begin with, a poor man does not leave property when he dies. His parents were not rich but he had made friends with very rich families. He left a very impressive library, so he could not have been all that ignorant. Thousands of years before Mohammed, Egyptians, (and long before them Phoenicians) build the most amazing constructions that to this day, modern scientists and architects do not understand how they could possibly have done it. Have you read Pythagoras? I knew a man in Wales, a retired locomotive driver, who never went to school and he had people from all over Britain going to him to solve their health problems. A man who's never seen a medical book in his life and totally un-educated anyway. But he had this power to heal, an instinctive knowledge of what's wrong with the person and what the person should do in order to get well.

The Indian doctor Deepak Chopra confessed that much of his ideas for curing came from flair. However, he, like other talented doctors or healers, are just happy to give to people, to help people, they just do it, without the need for God.

If you studied history and haven't forgotten it, you will know that Mohammed was a very ambitious young man. He couldn't, though, get an army by saying, 'I want to be powerful, I want to invade here, there, conquer these lands.'

The only way he could do it was by claiming he was doing it on behalf of God.

Remember that by the time Mohammed arrived, people had already been brainwashed for centuries with the notion that God was a kind monster who punished in the most cruel way those who disobey him. So, by following a religious leader, people were only doing it as a kind of insurance against what could happen to them.

You know and you could well teach others, about the history of terrorism. Reading through the original religious/history books, you can clearly see how terrorism has been practiced for thousands of years. Well before Islam existed.

People are prejudiced against something because they have been brainwashed but do not realize it. As Hitler said, 'How lucky for rulers, that people do not think'. He couldn't believe how easy it was to have almost an entire country change its way of thinking, simply because he had a big voice and knew how to choose his words during public speeches.

Ahed

You are so right when you say, 'the whole situation in the Arab World is so complicated. The people are so confused.'

This is precisely what Washington and London have been striving for, for 60 years, with the complicity of all the Arab sheiks, princes, kings and oil barons. And this situation does not exist in the Middle East only. You'll find it in Afghanistan, Pakistan, India, Nepal, Sri-Lanka, Bangladesh, Indonesia, etc.

You say, 'Our regimes in America are supportive of Israel', but, although I understand why you say it, from my point of view, they do not support Israel, they only support themselves.

Politicians always look at their personal interests first. In fact, oil-rich Arabic countries are equally 'supportive' of the mess in the countries I've just mentioned.

Also, you're so right when you speak about those regimes as having such 'control of all media that is talking about Israel as an enemy and saying, let's get ready for a war.' The Media is used internationally, to confuse people, to brainwash populations.

Two years ago, when Cherie Blair - wife of the then British Prime Minister, Tony Blair, spoke in a British University to a class of Journalism students, she said, 'You are preparing for one of the dirtiest professions around', 'dirty and dangerous'. Mrs Blair KNEW what she was talking about!

You have told me before that everything in the Arab World is based on lying or twisting the truth! I am trying to make you understand, my friend, that this is all part of the Game - a pre-requisite to creating conflicts, worldwide.

Ahed, with all the respect I have for you, I have to express my disagreement with your point of view. You say about the Zionist lobby: '......his success to divert the conflict between Israel and Arabs/Muslims to a conflict between America and Arabs/Muslims'.

I strongly disagree. To begin with, it is not 'the Zionist lobby', but the 'weapon lobby' or the 'Arms Trade', with Zionists, non-Zionists, Jews, Muslims, Christians, Hindus, all involved.

You forget that in America there are also powerful Muslims and you forget the strong business relationship between America and the Arab countries. That relationship would be much weaker without the Jews/Arab conflict.

Furthermore, the 'supposed' conflict between America and Arabs/Muslims is also desired by both the Arab lobby and Washington. You are obsessed with the Zionist lobby, but you completely neglect the work of the CIA, whose secret agents, like US diplomats, are paid to create conflicts.

Of course Ahed, we must look at the Zionist lobby, but we must also look at 'ALL' the lobbies. There are around 200 armed conflicts in the world today. Only one, Ahed, only one involves Jews. Please, look at the world around you !!!!

Alberto

29

THE WAY I SEE THINGS

It is all too easy to forget that 'ceasefire' is only another word for 'truce' - that is, a temporary stop of the violence. A pause that is just long enough for both sides to work out negotiations for re-starting the violence.

Those who think clearly will know that both sides in any conflict are guilty of killing others. Both sides in any conflict are fully aware, too, that violence is not going to take them anywhere but to more trouble and more crimes against humanity. Both sides will maintain – insist – that they work very hard to achieve peace. But their daily 'obligations' are how to kill and how to abuse the power they have. And here lies the problem: the TRUTH is, they do not have to 'work very hard.' Tragically, with modern weapons, killing is the simplest thing to do. Both sides in any conflict work for the powers above them. Killing, 'thanks' to the position of power, is the easiest thing to do, the easiest way of assuring success or 'victory'. What is difficult for a politician -and here, YES, he must work very hard - is, to achieve (if he 'really' wants it) - Peace.

Look at former British Prime Minister, Tony Blair. Had he resisted the orders by the universal powers to invade Iraq, he would not have become a multi-millionaire. Thanks to destroying Iraq, he helped kill almost a million Iraqi civilians, maim a further 3 million, and allow in the process, hundreds of British young men and women to die. He helped Bush's oil business, helped train Iraqis in the cultivation and production of drugs, and helped to destroy the economy of his own country. But he did manage to help himself. He bought twelve properties, two of them for the value of 8 million dollars. They are in various parts of England. One of the 8 million dollar houses is in Connaught Square, London, where he now resides. Ten are apartments, for his children and for further investment. The second 8 million dollar property was bought about two weeks ago. It is in the country. The house was home to the late great English actor, John Gielgud. This is where Tony Blair can go for a calm day in the countryside, whilst thousands of British citizens seek solace in the cemeteries, visiting the graves of those killed by Blair's wars.

All politicians will say that they are against wasting and destroying lives for no reason. Of course. But when they play war, they know that war is a game. And in the 'game of war' the winner is the one who kills the most, so players on both sides must play with that in mind. And the goal has to be for each participant to kill more than his adversary.

It is important to look carefully at the words we use, to analyse the meaning of our words. If we write, of Israel and Palestine, say, 'this ceasefire could lead to a move towards negotiations,' it implies we think Palestinian and Israeli leaders really work for Peace. Believe me, if Presidents or Prime Ministers really worked for Peace, they would not be sued, like Sharon, Olmert, Berlusconi, Putin, Bush, the late Milosevic and countless others, for corruption, fraud and money laundering. Their names and reputations are soiled because they are in the VERY DIRTY arms business. Arms in this case means also oil, gold, drugs and prostitution. The ONLY way out of this situation is to make it impossible for politicians to enter the dirty arms business in the first place. However, this can never happen while the world continues to invent, develop, manufacture and trade arms.

Look at all the wars in Latin America, Africa and Asia since the end of World War II. Around 200 armed conflicts in the world at any given moment, outside of Europe. The 'business' provided by World War II had to be transferred to other continents.

Look at the current British Prime Minister Gordon Brown. Does he 'also' want to take advantage of his power to become a multi-millionaire, just like his predecessor Tony Blair? He met with Bush, announcing two hours later that he was immediately sending another 200 soldiers to Afghanistan. He then announced that by this time next year, instead of 5,000 British troops, Afghanistan would have 8,000 of them. This, of course, resulted in a re- arming of the Taliban; to make sure the fighting (and the arms industry) can continue. This is the business - the patriotic un-written 'duty' - of Prime Ministers and Presidents.

Similar rules apply, also, to oil, gold and other precious commodities. Clinton's fortune came from drugs. The US now controls about 70% of drug production in Afghanistan and have initiated the Iraqi in the art and business of drug planting and cultivating. Margaret Thatcher made her fortune thanks to the warships business, albeit indirectly. It is well known that she introduced her son to the weapons business (through Saudi Arabia). This has also made him a multi-millionaire.

One way to make life easier for themselves - the politicians in power - is to make sure that the majority of people 'do not think'. This is why they want a 'drugged' society. They complement this with a promotion of stupid and often violent TV programmes, and games that produce ignorant and violent youth. There is also the political promotion of sports events. The bigger, the longer, the better. The Olympic Games are ideal for corrupt political leaders. They can go about organising weapon deals and transfers, as well as wars, with a tamed society too distracted by sports to notice what they plan and do. To me there are no 'black forces'. Everything is very white. Very clear.

It is often said when assessing conflict, politicians and their place in history that, 'only time will tell'. But we do not learn. The example of World War II, also applies to Israel/Palestine. Retired Israeli Army experts are already working in many countries of the world, whether in the weapon business, fighting in armies (official and mercenary), training guerrilla groups and terrorists. And these are only the 'retired' people ! If Israel had no more need for their Armed Forces, the world would be invaded by Israeli military officers seeking a job and promoting Israeli arms !!!!

Does my analysis assume that only the worst can happen? I frankly cannot see, how, once weapons are bought, people trained in their use, politicians ordering their use, anything other than war can happen. It is also true, for instance, that Egypt and Israel have not been killing each other for decades, and neither have Jordan and Israel for the same time. But what is the price of this? Many Americans and other nationals, tourists in Egypt have been killed. There have been bombs outside the pyramids, in Cairo hotels. Furthermore, it is thanks to Egypt and Jordan's Treaty with Israel, that Palestinians have such a terrible time.

Even Churches have guns and many of them invest in the arms industry. In England, 72 Universities invest in the weapon industries, about 50 of them are involved in weapon research and development and all the Universities with Peace Studies are involved in weapon research and development.

Look at Boston's world famous MIT, where the wonderful and equally famous Noam Chomsky lectures. They have a multi-million contract with the US Armed Forces, for the development of new materials, to make wars in the Arabian deserts more comfortable for American soldiers. Some are almost ready to be tried in Iran. MIT also studies on how soldiers could survive in a future nuclear war. MIT is also developing new material for air-fighters to fly at such heights that they'll be totally invisible and inaudible.

And this is only one among hundreds of Universities. In the USA almost half a million scientists receive their salaries and research funds from the US Military Budget. Weapon factories exist and prosper 'thanks' to academics at these Universities.

Consider the way Sir Hugh Orde, Head of the Police Service of Northern Ireland, described terrorism and how to stop it. It revealed that if politicians and Police had been doing the 'right thing' all along, we would have never had terrorism in the first place. Sir Hugh recommends, 'talking'. But why do we have terrorism? It is precisely 'because' of the kind of talking Sir Hugh suggests.

The real and effective talk should take place 'before' any terrorist organisation is born. But this is not what the elite that runs the world will allow, as Sir Hugh very well knows. On the contrary, talks go on in order to 'create' terrorism. Manuals on 'how to become a terrorist', with chapters on how to make bombs, how to kidnap people, torture hostages, how to extortionate hostage families, are all published with official knowledge and approval.

Everybody knows that Al Qaeda is in permanent talks with the UK and with Washington. In fact Al Qaeda was formed by the US, its soldiers trained in the US. Osama Bin Laden, like Saddam Hussein and so many others, were on the CIA payroll. When the Twin Towers collapsed in 2001, all US airports were shut down by the authorities, except for one that just opened to let the Bin Laden family fly out of the country. The Bin Laden and Bush families have had a fruitful business relationship for years. In fact, both are investors in Carlyle, the biggest American weapon conglomerate, now represented in Europe by former UK Prime Minister John Major.

There are educated political journalist and historians, particularly in the Middle East, whose bodies and minds have been tortured and twisted for decades, who have seen with their own eyes the most horrific human tragedy imaginable. Injustice that no words can describe fully.

I have been to Israel several times and am witness to the small but powerful anti-Palestinian lobby. However, I do not blame them for their strident views. They are all victims of the brainwashing of foreign powers and the secret agents the powers need, so that there is never Peace. Peace is bad for business for the elite that runs the world.

In reality, a 'Jewish' state of Israel should have never been created. At least not in Palestine. But if the world was run by Peace-seekers, we would never have had World War I and II, the Holocaust, Pol Pot, Pinochet, and a myriad of other cruel dictators and cruel wars

Sadly, the Peace-loving masses of the world have to endure war after war, to serve the interests of the small minority who control us. But I do not think that my message has no hope in it. To me, it is exactly the opposite. I write, write and write and ....write, that Peace in the world can exist. But any hope for Peace whilst making wars, talking about war, agonising about which side holds the moral high-ground, staging militaristic memorials to 'heroes'- those who killed the most or were killed during fighting, producing, selling and using arms, is the same as hope for tropical weather in Alaska. An oxymoron.

Dear Ahed,

What telepathy!!! You write to me on the very day you are in my mind for hours, as I am in the final pages of my book, 'Dear Ahed' -The Game of War and the Path to Peace. By absolute coincidence, I was just writing to explain the reason for the book's title and who you are.

It is exactly as you say, 'Obama, McCain, Bush, or anyone else, must accomplish every and each task or mission already on his desk.' And he, Obama, is fulfilling them.

Sadly, one of the tasks before Obama is that he must maintain and increase the tension between Palestine and Israel. By his long meeting with the AIPAC people and the words he uttered in Amman, he can report to his paymasters 'mission accomplished'.

You correctly report that, 'Obama promised to stay away from, and to block, lobbyists in the White House'. To me, after many years of listening to political jargon, to politicians pronouncing such inaccuracies, simply to fool the world at the same time as becoming better loved by the masses, it only means that, instead of lobbyists and politicians meeting in the Pentagon, in the White House or one of the Five-Star-hotels they use, to combine business with pleasure, politicians and their 'business partners' (the lobbyists) will carry on with their activities in more discreet places.

Ahed, you say you hope 'Obama will work harder on saving lives among Arabs, Israelis and others.' But there are no 'others'. Do talk to weapon manufacturers and they will tell you that I am saying the truth and nothing but the truth.

If weapons stopped killing Palestinians and Israelis, the bullets and bombs would be used on other victims. This is the rule, the law of the Game. We must get rid of this game. There is no other Path to Peace.

With all good wishes,

Alberto

30

IN THE BEGINNING IS THE END

T S Eliot wrote that what we call the beginning is often the end. It is so in my own life: *'The end'* has been and is my work for peace. It is from where I started in this book. I want to explain my passion, outline my awaking to the problems leading to war, from where it started.

Friends have been nagging me for months to write a book. A book with my ideas about the world, its history, the present and the way forward, if we are to achieve what the majority of inhabitants of our beautiful planet Earth, really want: to live in a Peaceful and Just world. Not only a warless world, but also one that is free from hunger and pollution.

Much has been written about the past, but history is just that: history; and history cannot be changed. We can only 'use' the past to understand the present and we can analyse the present to understand why the world is the way it is and where it is going. We can then see what we, the occupants of this planet, could do to change its course.

Basically, through the collection of thoughts in this book, I have tried to explain the fundamental reasons why, despite the fact that the vast majority of the human population - and I do not exaggerate if I say 99.9% - want Peace but Peace cannot be because of the tiny minority that wants War, is very powerful, TOO powerful and it is this minority, sadly that decides the course of events.

To explain how I have arrived at the position I hold on matters of war, peace and governance, I need to explain two details. Firstly, I need to tell you about Ahed, the man whom you have met throughout these pages and whose name forms the title of the book. He is a Palestinian, once caught physically and still caught up emotionally in the tragedy of the Middle East. He is now residing in the United States of America: Ahed Hussein.

Ahed and I have exchanged many letters, discussed many things. I have written to him letters of moral support and letters on a variety of topics, in which I discuss with him the problems of Palestine and Israel via 'Peace & Dialogue', the

Internet Forum dedicated to Middle Eastern problems. We have never met personally, but we know each other well.

The second 'detail' is my own background. If you have read the notes at the start of this book, or glanced at the dust cover, you will already know that I was born in La Plata, the capital of Buenos Aires province, in Argentina, 60kms. South of Buenos Aires City, the capital of Argentina.

My family was a mixture of various nationalities and origins. On my father's side, his family - all his living siblings included - arrived in Argentina from Romania. Hundreds of years earlier, his ancestors had lived in Holland and Portugal.

My mother was born in Argentina, but her own mother was also from Romania and her father from Russia, although his own family was originally from Germany.

Through marriages, I have had and still have, Polish, Lithuanian, Israeli, Turkish, Brazilian and American relatives.

Argentina itself is a hotchpotch of every possible nationality in the world, in addition to the original citizens of Latin American, dating back many thousands of years. The only shortfall in Argentina was of people of African origin, but that was made up by our neighbouring country Brazil.

I can truly say that in the first years of my life, due to my family background, the country I grew up in, and later, from my travels around the world as a musician, I have met people from almost every nationality, ethnic group, religion and skin colour.

As part of my music studies and later the first years of my professional career, I lived for nearly seven years in Geneva, Switzerland. This charming town being the home of the European headquarters of the United Nations, International Labour Organization, International Red Cross and various other important and influential bodies, afforded me the opportunity to complete what I call my 'universal' education. I think that by the time I left Geneva for London, I had met every possible variation of the human being, except an Eskimo.

From an intellectual point of view, my mind and heart also had the perfect opportunity to develop and understand 'universality'. This came through my music studies, not only the playing of the piano and the conducting, but also through the study and listening of the music of most countries on the planet.

I experienced so many wars. So much conflict. Saw such suffering. Why, in spite of so many peace initiatives, was there never peace anywhere for long? We, human beings, are all equal. No matter in which country we are born, who our parents are, which religion they impose on us, which language we learn to speak, what food we eat, what colour our skin is, we are all equal. It suddenly clicked. No matter which way I turned the arguments I knew fully that no matter who our parents or educators are, which religion our family or educators impose on us, we are all members of this unique race known as 'the human race' and that we all are equal.

It was in Geneva that I also became aware of the manipulation of the world by powerful groups. Powerful businesses, powerful families, including a few 'royal' families, powerful bankers, powerful Churches and the powerful Media.

It was also in Geneva that I realized how little power politicians - and by extension, diplomats, have, and how they all depend on the groups I have just mentioned. Not only do they 'depend' on them, but also they actually have to 'obey' them and carry out their wishes.

It was also in Geneva that I noticed that politicians who 'do not obey', are made to disappear off the scene. Sometimes by removing them from power, sometimes by destroying their political careers, sometimes by straightforward murder.

But the most interesting revelation came to me a few months after my arrival in Switzerland. In those days, my late teens, I was not interested in politics and the name 'United Nations' meant absolutely nothing to me. I did not even bother to enquire as to what United Nations, or ' l'ONU', as it was called in French, meant or did.

However, as a starving young student, I had to work and although my first interest was in finding children to whom I could teach piano, in the first months I had to accept all kind of jobs, from baby-sitting to house/flat cleaning, from messenger boy to kitchen porter. It was in the course of these duties that I met people, many of them foreigners, who worked at or had some connection with the United Nations.

Once I started to teach piano and Spanish, I met more UN employees. Some were local employees; others were diplomats, representing their country, employed by their country.

I became curious as to what these people from around the world were all doing in Geneva, all working in the same building. I have always been interested in people so, with time, I became quite friendly with several diplomats, from all corners of the globe. The more I knew them, the more conversations we had about their work, the more my eyes opened. The more they told me about their work, their gains, their frustrations, the pressure, the more I became convinced that diplomats working at the United Nations were not working for the sake of Peace but for the financial benefit of their country and the politicians who had sent them to Geneva. In fact, I often had the impression that these diplomats were working 'against' their country, against their country's interests.

One of the details that made a strong impression on me, were the negotiations that made these diplomats happy, while I knew these very negotiations which so lifted their spirits, were going to result in their country being at war - civil war or a war with a neighbouring country. It bewildered me.

When I celebrated my birthday in Geneva for the first time, several of the cards I received carried the following message (in different guises) 'Alberto, how lucky you are, living in the town that hosts the organisation that protects the world from wars'. Such words did not make sense to me. I asked my friends to explain. Without exception, my friends explained fervently, to my disbelieving mind, 'The United Nations, my friend, the organisation created to make sure the world does not have any more wars.'

I thought my old friends were all crazy, sarcastic or drunk when they wrote to me in this fashion! After months in Switzerland, observing the work of my newly made friends and acquaintances, comparing what I read in the Press about UN activities with what they told me they had been doing, I could only conclude that the United Nations had been created as a kind of 'Club of Nations'. I was told by so many people that the UN was to protect the world from war. It was not what I was seeing first hand.

From my observations, this 'club' – and I can only call it that - had been set up to promote business and it seemed that everybody that I got to know who was involved in it agreed that the best and foremost business, for all concerned parties, was the weapon business, the Arms Trade. And with a slow realisation, I became horribly aware that all the people within this 'club' seemed to agree that if wars were necessary, for the business, then, so be it. Let's have a war was the tacit message. .I hasten to add that I have also met diplomats who were wonderful human beings.

What struck me next, was the inequality of the negotiations between rich, developed, advanced countries and countries belonging to what was then known as the 'Third World' or 'developing' countries in need of help. By 'inequality', I mean the gain to the country. Relative to this, to the personal gains of the diplomats themselves, the inequality wasn't very noticeable.

But what struck me most of all, a truly shocking and depressing discovery, was the fact that diplomats were doing most of the time the opposite from what they told the world. I had always heard that diplomats were there to do the job politicians were incapable of doing. However, after a few months in contact and developing friendships with U.N. diplomats and other U.N. staff, I realized many diplomats were in reality part of the spying world.

Of course, it did not take me long to understand this once I realised their salaries were being paid by their Government, so their obligations and duties were first and foremost to their Government, or paymasters. They had to negotiate what was better financially for them as well as for the country they represented, regardless.

Unfortunately for the innocent billions of citizens in the world, what 'was better' was always measured in figures, in money. How much for you, how much for me. Negotiations so often involved weapon deals, loans to poor countries were often conditioned by weapon deals, that there was a point in my life in Geneva when I could predict with respectable accuracy wars that were going to break in the world.

The longer I lived in Geneva, the stronger my belief and conviction the United Nations was used for arranging wars. I also noticed that the United States of America was doing its utmost to promote the Arms Trade in countries where weapons were very likely to be used - and they carefully planned wars in countries as far as possible from the US.

I always felt that had Cuba been in Vietnam and vice versa, nearly 70,000 US soldiers would have died in Cuba and Kennedy and Kruschev would have negotiated the avoidance of war in Vietnam.

Being very fond of the French language, I tried my best to improve it. However, with a few Spanish-speaking colleagues at the Music Conservatoire and 80% of my friends at the UN from Spain or Latin America, I did not have much chance to make good progress in French.

My landlady - I was renting a small room in her flat - a well educated woman, advised me to practice through becoming familiar with the daily language used by journalists, that is, to listen to the news on the radio and to read newspapers. This WAS a discovery!

The more I read or heard the news reported by the Media, the more I realized how inaccurate the news was. At the beginning, I stupidly accused journalists of ignorance and sometimes of being simply straightforward liars.

However, as time went by, I gradually awoke to the truth. Journalists were genuinely, in all sincerity, reporting what they had heard from UN politicians/diplomats. The problem was that they did not seem to be aware that politicians were not telling them the truth - or rather, not the full truth - of their activities within the UN.

In my conversations with people working at the United Nations, not necessarily politicians or diplomats, but also with translators and interpreters, I would hear one thing about a particular subject and then, on the wireless, I would hear something different, on the same subject.

In the beginning, I would innocently question my friends, saying, 'You told me this - but in the newspaper I read **this**' The usual reply was, 'Well Alberto, **this** I cannot reveal to the world but only to close friends.' Double standards were the norm widely accepted by everyone.

In my years in Geneva, close to the United Nations, I saw several diplomats become very rich, not from the salaries they received from their respective Government, but from the negotiations they masterminded. Sadly, most of those negotiations involved weapons. I mean everything military: arms, tanks, air-fighters, warships, the lot.

By following world events in the Media, I came to see how so many of those military negotiations were connected, directly or indirectly, to armed conflicts in the world. This is what led me to continue my investigations into the patterns governing politicians and diplomats, not only in my new home, in London, but in all countries of the world that I visited for my work as a musician.

A few years later, still thinking, 'How innocent these journalists are believing everything politicians tell them', I discovered how wrong I was. Journalists - though not all of them - are very enlightened people. They know very well they are not being told the truth or the full truth. However, the Press barons who are their employers and paymasters compel them to report from the briefings they are given.

More years passed and I met several political journalists. The more I spoke with them, the more I realised how they were often not true to themselves when they wrote or published. Their writing was of necessity influenced by two main considerations: the political interests of whoever owned the publication they were working for and how strong their wish to remain employed by the newspaper they were writing for.

In journalism, the strongest proof of hypocrisy I saw (you could also call it 'cynicism' or 'following the newspaper's agenda') was when I read a journalist in a Right wing paper and later in a Left-wing publication, or vice versa.

I found in the world of Politics not just hypocrisy, but true 'Comedy'. In the beginning of my 'awakening' years, little did I suspect that all those rants and insults between politicians belonging to opposing parties were just showmanship. The first time I happen to share a table with two such political 'enemies', I found that not only were they excellent friends, but that they agreed on almost every political issue discussed over the meal. I suddenly understood the career role of the politician. They are bound to the supposed ideology of the Party to which they belong, as slaves were - and still are - bound. Non-slaving politicians, as was the case of Thatcher's Housing Minister, Ian Gow, meet with tragic ends, to their career or life. In many countries, I have seen politicians change parties as one changes the route to work or a brand of cigarettes.

Anyway, coming to the 'reason' for this book and explain my anti-militaristic stance, I shall start by saying that since my early days in Geneva, I asked myself, 'Has the world not had enough with World War II? (It was only 15 years after the end of World War II when I arrived in Geneva). Have politicians not learnt a lesson from this tragic experience and catastrophe for the world?'

Well, the longer I stayed in Switzerland, the more I read, the more people I met, including some millionaire families, several of them in Banking, the more I asked questions, received replies, the more it became obvious to me, that there were so many people who had so vastly benefited from the war, that the last thing they wanted was a world without wars.

Their only concern was, '.... but we've had enough in Europe; let's organize wars away from us'. So, I started to see the projecting of wars in Latin America, but mainly in African countries and in South-East Asia.

This was the early Sixties when I gained the impression that several of the countries that joined the United Nations Club during its first decade had come to their experienced colleagues, to ask for help in organizing wars, against other countries or between themselves.

To put it in very simple terms, Britain, the US, and other powers, would convince an African country the solution to their problems was war or to change a lay Government for a military dictatorship. If a country already had a military Government in place, the UN powers would still find ways of convincing diplomats that revolution to get rid of their dictator was necessary. If there were ethnic problems, religious problems or disputes over lands, that was very good news for the UN community. It meant they could promote the Arms Trade. This 'trade' benefited certain countries, certain politicians and diplomats.

I had become so aware of this miserable situation, which always resulted in hundreds, or thousands dead and millions of pounds, Swiss francs or dollars wasted, that I could predict, based on the degree of happiness and rise in living standards of an Ambassador or diplomat to the United Nations, when and where a war was going to erupt. So, to me, the United Nations was an organisation whose mission was to create wars, but pretending the opposite. Of course, everybody thought I was mad !!!!

However, I have had plenty of opportunities since those days, to prove myself right and sane.

The United Nations had a High Commission for Human Rights. I read and studied well the Universal Declaration of Human Rights. Every single Article of the Declaration was constantly abused by so many countries, but the UN Commission did - and still does - nothing about it. To give you just one example: the Declaration says that all children must have an education. In the Sixties, when I lived in Geneva, Cambodia was already a member of the UN - since 14th December 1955 - but had no compulsory education for children and still does not have it, in 2008!

However, the United Nations have made it possible for the Cambodian regime of Pol Pot to slaughter nearly 2 million people. In most cases, humiliating deaths preceded by agonising torture.

If I start writing on Human Rights abuses 'promoted' by the United Nations, I shall never finish this book. So I will tell you about another of my observations. The Swiss prided themselves of being pacifists and 'neutral', but thought joining the United Nations was not for them.

I soon realized why. Neutrality allowed them to do 'double' business, as they could sell weapons to both warring factions.

Dear Ahed,

I am very happy to read your wise, enlightened and mature words.

Just for your information, my family escaped from Eastern Europe, between 1935 and 1940. Those who did not, perish either in the gas chambers, as victims of manual torture, (burnt, buried alive) or of mechanical torture (bullets, bombs, etc) died from starvation and some died of simple heart attacks, produced by the horrors they saw.

I grew up with all this horror. Not one day of my childhood went by without my father telling us some of the most gruesome details of what the war did to him and to his family. About 70% of the family was killed. Until the day he died, aged 80, he would frequently wake up in the middle of the night in a desperate, agitated and frightened state, as a result of a nightmare, scenes from his adolescence that were implanted into his mind and spirit.

Now to your points. You say, 'I never blamed Israel/Jews alone for our suffering in Palestine. I can repeat that Arabs/Muslims should take the first blame.'

But what I am saying to you is that 'not only' Arabs/Muslims or Israel/Jews are to be blamed. On the contrary, those two people are the least responsible. We should not forget that the Cambodian, Vietnamese, Angolan, Lebanese or Afghan massacres and Civil Wars, would have never occurred, had it been left to the people of those countries. Those wars occurred because the USA and Russia playing a game invented by the Vatican, called The Cold War.

The Cold War is the bloodiest game ever created by the Vatican - designed by the Society of Jesus, otherwise known as Jesuits. Coincidentally, not long ago, an Argentinean ex-Jesuit priest, now married and father of two lovely children wrote a book, alas not yet translated to English, called, *'The Unhappy Catholic.'* The book explains quite accurately the sinister plans and activities of the Vatican, which prompted the writer to quit the 'Firm' or the 'Company'.

In your second point, you say, 'America, Canada, West Europe are the most powerful countries.' It is true, but they are powerful because a) they are the main weapon producers in the world and b) because they follow Vatican instructions. When a country does not do that, like the case of Venezuela, with a President (Chavez) who continually criticizes the Vatican, you are in trouble. Look at assassinated President Kennedy, a Catholic himself. He had plans that were going to remove power from the Vatican, so he had to go. Jesuits instructions are very clear. Even if it is one of us, if he plans things that are not beneficial to our organisation, it is perfectly legal and acceptable, to get rid of him'.

You also say, 'I know very well how much the Soviets helped Israel with more than half of its population,' but this is your personal perspective. For Russia, it was simply an excellent way of ridding itself from those Jews they hated. The 'last' thing they had in mind was to help Israel. Also in those days of little food in Russia, the Soviets were very happy to have fewer mouths to feed.

I am very sorry that you do not see that 'your' problem is also the problem of the Bosnians and many others. You forget the Church is ONE. Wherever there are Muslims, they all belong to the same group and the same goes for Catholics. It is the two Churches that are at war. The different countries on which they play their game, is incidental.

It is just like two champion chess players or two champion footfall teams. They can one day play their game in Los Angeles, the next game in Istanbul, the next in Kuala Lumpur, the next in Melbourne, ad infinitum. The location changes, but the players do not.

I hope you understand this. It is very important.

With my warmest good wishes,

Alberto

31

THE GAME

'War is a continuation of Diplomacy by other means.' Otto von Bismark

Former Chief Economist of the World Bank and Nobel Memorial Prize winning economist, Joseph Stiglitz has written in his book (with Linda Blimes), 'The Trillion Dollar War', that the Iraq war, estimated to cost between 50 and 60 billion dollars, actually cost three trillion dollars. That is twelve zeros! He draws the analogy that the 5 billion dollars given in aid to Africa equals just ten days fighting costs and 8 days of fighting costs equals a year of aid to Africa. Where the Bush Administration had expected a quick and inexpensive conflict, there is an ongoing war, which has already cost more than the twelve-year war in Vietnam and is projected to cost some ten times the cost of the previous Iraq war. And the war has been financed solely by borrowing.

But this is not only what wars cost. The costs to society will not be shown in the budgets. There is an ongoing social and moral cost, hidden by the mendacious use of language - the lies, the deception of those in the power elite.

Meditating for Peace cannot win over the 150 million of the human race who have a compulsion for, and business needs for war.

These include University students and teachers, plus all professional scientists who work on weapon research and development, the owners and employees of factories around the world, producing guns, cannons, tanks, air, land and sea missiles, grenades, mortars, landmines, torture instruments, spying devices, armoured cars, war helicopters, warships, air-fighters, nuclear submarines, soldier uniforms, professional military, and those traditional nationalists who stand for one country only.

This industry of war in turn produces a fortune for Churches, Press Barons. Politicians, Banks, Banking families. Royal families and military chiefs. A fortune, but also power and a place in history.

This is why despite the billions around the world who already meditate, chant, pray or march for peace in their millions world wide, we never see Peace. The Dalai Llama has said that he personally believes that war cannot ever lead to the ultimate solution. *'Voicing one's opposition to war alone is not enough,'* he stresses. *'We must do something to bring about an end to war and conflict, and one of the things we have to think about is disarmament. We must make serious efforts to achieve disarmament[2]'.* But big business, the arms manufactures, do not want disarmament. The 'Powers' do not want Peace.

Political parties exist so that people believe they live in a Democracy. Wonderful illusion that allows politicians to become rich, rob, steal, create conflicts, internal or with other countries. The Romans said 'Divide and Rule'. This is what the powers want: a 'divided society'. The more political parties you have, the better. It means groups become smaller and weaker. This is why Israel has so many problems and cannot solve any. They have almost 30 parties. Mad !!!!

---

[2] The Art of Living

Basically all parties are all the same. Beware however, of a party, like the Nepali Congress, which says; 'Sovereignty and state power shall rest on the people'. This is the biggest lie that politicians utter in all countries of the world. The 'People' have no sovereignty, let alone State power. This is why 'patriotism' is taught. It is taught so that 'The People' feel they 'must' obey the State, in order to be good citizens.

I work actively for Peace, for Human Rights, for Justice and the Environment. I do not have faith in the anti nuclear weapons lobby because at the moment, 80% of the current damage done to our environment comes from the testing and use of conventional weapons, 80% of workers in the War Industry work in conventional weapons factories. Conventional weapons are so developed and powerful, in part because of the anti-nuclear lobby. Those scientists - the inventors of the conventional weapon, - have escaped the pressure of publicity and demonstrations and have, in effect, been left free to kill the world with these ever more sophisticated weapons. Sophisticated conventional weapons of today are almost as lethal as the nuclear variety.

Stop the War Campaign groups, like Abolition of War, are all the same, always campaigning on the basis of how terrible all these lives lost and the cost to the economy. Two items that do not interest politicians in the least. Those in power will never be touched by these arguments.

Militarism is MILITARISM, the world over. There is NO COUNTRY IN THE WORLD where torture and the most despicable, inhumane atrocities are not committed. I live in England, one of the several countries in the world producing torture instruments. Do you think they manufacture them especially for Israel to use on Palestinians? Manufacturers would go bankrupt!

And you expect a military to treat the prisoner in a humane way? A military? Someone who chose to be paid for killing people as a career? Someone who had to study and pass exams on torture? What difference does it make, dying from torture or dying because the roof of your house fell on you, after it was hit by a bomb thrown from the skies? What about if the bomb doesn't kill you and you are left with half a leg, and four broken ribs? Is that really not as bad as 'prison torture'? ONLY an end to militarism IS THE SOLUTION. There is no ALTERNATIVE.

The poorest countries in the world, where children have no schools, no food, no clothes, no medical care, have Armed Forces. Thousands in Pakistan do not have enough to eat, yet their Government buys three brand new warships, equipped with Excocets et al. Wars are making so much money for politicians that that is what counts. If the country goes bankrupt, it's not their problem. As individuals, they retire or are ousted and new people will come to clean up the mess.

Human lives will become a concern of politicians only when the law establishes that the politician who decides on war, must send to the front line his own children and other relatives and only if these people are killed should they be allowed to send innocent victims to continue the fight.

I work for Human Life, against the millions of unnecessary and untimely deaths we have every year, through wars, lack of food or medical care.

Ahed and his siblings, thanks to a sensitive, intelligent and educated father, belong to the 'majority' of Palestinians, who, despite how bad the loss of their country feels for them, were never aware of any anti-Jewish feelings. Ahed's father taught his son that those Jews coming to Israel were greater victims than the Palestinians. He made Ahed read articles or books about the Holocaust.

Ahed's father, as the enlightened man he was, knew Britain and other powers were to blame for the suffering of Muslims and Jews in modern history.

If I had 10 billion dollars, I would use them to educate the world, to stop the education of patriotism, nationalism and religious bigotry. To close all weapon factories and disband all Armed Forces, creating new jobs for all of the new unemployed.

This would put an end to the shameful 5 million children who die in our world because of lack of food, plus another 3 million who die because of lack of medical care. It would also end with the Third World, with all humanity, living as one big loving family.

We cannot seek the truth about our world or get accurate information from the media or the press. There **is** no independent press. No journalists can write the full truth.

There is a much-quoted story, attributed to John Swinton, (1829-1901) who was managing editor at The New York Times during the time of the Civil War. When guest of honour at a banquet, speaking on the independence of the press he apparently said, '*There is no such thing, at this day in the world's history, in America, as an independent Press. You know it and I know it. There is not one of you who dares to write your honest opinions, and if you did, you know beforehand that it would never appear in print. I am paid weekly for keeping my honest opinion out of the paper I am connected with. Others of you are paid similar salaries for similar things, and any of you who would be so foolish as to write honest opinions, would be out on the street looking for another job. If I allowed my honest opinion to appear in one issue of my paper, before twenty-four hours my occupation would be gone. You know it and I know it. And what folly is this - toasting an independent Press? We are all tools and vassals of rich men behind the scenes. We are the jumping jacks, they pull the strings and we dance. Our talents, our possibilities and our lives are all the property of other men. We are intellectual prostitutes.*' This story is often quoted in varying forms. I repeat it here because the dreadful kernel of truth within these words is particularly relevant today. Politics has to be served.

Politics is a game and a game needs opponents. The same way that a chess player cannot win or lose a game without an opponent; a football team cannot win or lose without opposing team; an Army cannot win or lose wars without conflict. And politicians cannot win without wars, which to many of them only means business.

All the powerful forces know that they have to prove that they work for Peace and in order to do that they have to create wars first. They create fear so that they can protect us. They must pretend they want to end poverty, so they do everything they can to create it in the first place.

It is all a game that costs us our lives.

Dear Ahed,

Today I have had an email saying, **'The Gaza crisis has exploded. Put your name to our emergency petition demanding a ceasefire. We'll deliver it immediately to the UN Security Council, the Arab League, the US and other world leaders!'**

What can I say? The UN Security Council is made up of people and countries that favour, promote, the Israel/Palestine conflict. They are all in the business. They are all in the Game.

Reading the petition, I get even more depressed.

People have been - and obviously still are - brainwashed into believing Democracy exists and that politicians do what the 'people' ask them to do.

Reading the petition, I have this nightmarish vision of thousands, millions of people around the world, signing a petition, 2 months ago, to the UN, to the Israeli and

Palestinian Governments, to the military, saying to them, 'Please, we the undersigned, thousands of us, ask the relevant authorities to start a war between Israel and Palestine. We urge War Envoy Tony Blair (now disguised as Peace Envoy), to arrange the finances of Palestine, so that the Palestinian Authority can buy lots of rockets to send into Israel to provoke an Israeli response. Furthermore, we ask you not to stop the war before killing a few hundred people and causing the destruction of many buildings.'

ONLY WHEN PEOPLE WILL OPEN THEIR EYES AND MINDS, AND REALISE 'WHY' WE HAVE WARS AND 'WHO WANTS THEM', WILL A PETITION HAVE ANY REASON FOR BEING MADE.

It sometimes seems to me as if the media and peace commentators like to see the Palestinian people being attacked, wounded and killed by the Israeli, and Palestinian homes and other buildings been destroyed by bulldozers or bombs! The warfare stimulates protest and gives journalists and peace groups something to be furious about, something to write about, shout about.

However, the fact that out of this human and material tragedy some Palestinian and Israeli politicians are making lots of money for themselves, just the way Arafat and Sharon did earlier in the history of the region, does not seem to create the least concern.

When I suggested protest against the appointment of War Envoy Tony Blair, the warmonger and war criminal, who was the former British Prime Minister, no one wanted to know. Through a mass protest at Blair's appointment, many lives could have been saved. Such a protest would have been not so much against Tony Blair, but against the plan of the Illuminati, the Bankers who rule the world.

J P Morgan is possibly paying USA$ 500,000 a year to Tony Blair, to enable him to accomplish his criminal mission, which includes arranging financial assistance to Palestine. The official, allied corporate press will ultimately report that the decision was made, thanks to Blair's intervention, to help Palestine reach a better economy, to give its citizens a better life.

The un-official Truth - and I repeat that I told you this when Blair was appointed - is that the money had and has to be spent by Palestinians on rockets and other terror or murderous instruments - anything they can buy and use against Israel, anything that will infuriate even more the already furious Israelis.

So everything is going according to plan, to the delight of rocket manufacturers and many others who work in the Death Industry. As always, the Vatican is delighted too. Muslims and Jews killing each other is the best news they could hear. Muslims and Jews are delighted too, because, as on other occasions, they have ruined the festivities of the Christian world. As the world is run at the moment, the ceasefire will occur when the Banks want it to happen.

Alberto.

32

THE PATH FOR PEACE

If you manufacture shoes, freezers, cars, clothes or whatever, and you do not sell them, you cannot pay your employees, your taxes, or anything else that needs to be paid. You cannot, furthermore, renew your stock. In other words, your business goes bankrupt.

Exactly the same applies to manufacturers of guns, rifles, tanks, air fighters, missiles, uniforms for soldiers, torture equipment, and all other war commodities. Let us take any weapon manufacturing country as an example, say Switzerland. The Swiss Armed Forces are very well equipped, but the country is not at war, so how can manufacturers of warfare survive? And how can the Swiss Government create wealth? They would have to arm other countries. To do that they would have to create conflict. All countries are already armed. Governments will buy more if there is the prospect of war. Furthermore, if they do manage to go to war, better for business, as they have to keep buying.

As time goes by, factories of the country in question have developed better weapons, which have to go first to their own armed forces but the old weapons have not been used and the law of economics does not allow for those weapons, fighter planes, and other expensive war hardware, to be destroyed. So the government of that country has to officially or unofficially sell everything it has in store. Officially, they sell to friendly countries. That is, countries which are not at war, only improving the quality of their war material and countries who are at, or are planning, war, but are not going to use the weapons against the country that sold those weapons in the first place. When a poor country is asking for a loan of say 100 million pounds to build motorways, schools or hospitals, the loan is granted on condition that a large proportion of that money is used for purchasing war equipment. Governments count on Banks and other financial institutions to act as moneylenders and brokers to complete deals. This way, the promotion of wars is possible. However, although wars are very good for the pockets and Bank accounts of politicians, monarchs, Bank owners or top managers and weapon manufacturers, they are bad business for economies, particularly in poor countries.

This IS the current world economic crisis. It is nothing to do with sub-prime mortgages, as Governments would like us to believe. It is all to do with wars.

Unofficially, because there is a lot to be sold, there is the need to sell to 'unfriendly' countries as well, which means countries with which confrontation is possible. Like now, we make sure that the Taliban and Iraqi insurgents are well armed. Customers must be found. These customers often are countries of military dictators or military regimes, as was the case of Pol Pot in Cambodia and Pinochet in Chile. Thanks to the 'law of business', we also help the formation of child armies, militia groups and criminal organisations – mafias and terrorists. A president or government who is likely to be killing lots of people because of his ideology, madness or lust for power, is good news for so called 'democratic countries. There are countries where war can be incited, usually between neighbouring countries, or sometimes within a particular country creating civil wars. This happens often with the support (encouragement even) of the various churches. The more religious a Head of State, the more likely his country will fight wars. The weapon-manufacturing lobby is also very strong, with many politicians involved, and often churches as well.

Commercial attachés and, even more, military attachés of many countries are very busy instigating firearms businesses. Promoting 'guerrillas' is a way of finding clients as well as provoking general unrest and fear in society.

The situation is helped tremendously by the media, with newspapers, radio and TV stations carefully planning what they publish, say or show, so that they can brainwash readers, listeners and viewers. From creating a mild indisposition between two groups of people to developing extremist ideologies and outright wars.

Of course, it starts with media tycoons or editors having been brainwashed themselves first by politicians, religious leaders or conflict seekers. Vested interests also play an important role; several of the largest media corporations are owned by weapon manufacturers.

Of course I support 'Abolition 2000', for the destruction of all nuclear warfare, but I support more profoundly the Hague Appeal for Peace, which concerns itself with total universal disarmament. Reductions and eventually total abolition of small calibre guns in the hands of ordinary citizens should go with an equally gradual education of society to create a citizenship who, as adults, would consider war as totally unacceptable and propose that arms factories are closed down, their personnel given alternative jobs.

Apart from weapons, it is important to add that I would also recommend the universal ban of drugs for recreation. I hate the current comedy of Governments promoting anti-drugs agencies whilst encouraging, supporting and advising the citizens of Columbia or Afghanistan, to mention just two of the many countries, on how to increase production.

Governments of drug growing countries make it possible for workers to earn more working on a coca field than on wheat, fruit or flower field. Workers are also encouraged to become cocaine addicts so that they do not wish for a change.

I know the abolition of recreational drugs is easier said than done, because of vested interests, and because there are many drug consumers in positions of authority the world over. Vested interests because through official drug barons, there are politicians, as well as those working in the import/export of the drugs, who make a lot of money. Many politicians give lip service to abolition and say, 'We must stop the consumption of illegal drugs', when in reality, they do not really wish it to stop.

Going back to weapons both conventional and of mass destruction, it is said that to eliminate these weapons no government can act unilaterally but need the introduction of controls, so that there is no killing, maiming or terrorizing of their peoples, thus creating the institutional framework for peace. All I can see in this is the usual pattern: the introduction of new controls; all it does is create new loopholes, new black markets. It stimulates the creation of new and more sophisticated ways of smuggling. The person or country that made the weapon not only wants but also NEEDS to sell it, and the person or country that buys it NEEDS to use it, so that more needs to be bought, for more commission.

Religious education should stress that all people are the same, and we are all one family. Respect for the sanctity of life is to be practiced by all of us. For a Hindu to kill a Moslem, a Moslem to kill a Jew, a Catholic to kill a Protestant (all this in vice-versa as well) is like killing your own brother, your mother, your child, because we, the human race, are all brothers.

There would not be wars if the Human Rights organizations imposed on Governments the Right To Life of every citizen and reminded religious leaders that every member of their church has also got a Right to Life. This would mean that the President of a country would not have the right to send his citizens to die in a war, or even a small conflict, with another country. Even professional fighters and mercenaries could not exist in such a country. At most I would suggest that if war must be, then it should be 'performed' like a joust - just a small fight between the presidents concerned, or the heads of churches in conflict. And this, in any case, should be voted for by the citizens, as it should be in a democratic world. I bet if this were the case, there would never be another war!

I envisage a summit of responsible states where a meeting of Leaders of State could discuss without reserve issues of common concern, and where they could develop a sense of shared responsibility. First, however, a list should be drawn of the qualities a country should possess before being admitted as a 'responsible' state. The list should include all details of what a country has done to stop or prevent wars, social unrest, hunger, ill health, and deterioration of the environment. Any country wishing to qualify as a Responsible Country should also show what efforts are being made for building schools to improving teaching methods - ensuring the equal education of all its citizens. To qualify for membership to this elite, a country that is powerful, produces and sells weapons, should commit itself to the stopping of production and sale of the same. Equally, a country that buys weapons should be committed to the abolition of its armed forces.

A deep commitment to peace in the world and the happiness of all humanity, which implies no first and third worlds, but balance in the distribution of material wealth and knowledge, would also be a prerequisite to be accepted at this 'summit'! The only, and I repeat, only, people who should carry firearms will be the local, national and international police. I recognise that guns can, on occasions, be useful weapons. All the policeman needs to do is shoot in the legs rather than a fatal part of the body of a fast running criminal. When trying to prevent robbers, thieves and gangsters, including drug smugglers and pushers, from escaping arrest, stun guns should be the preferred method used, limiting the damage suffered by the escapee. International gun production would be solely for the use of the police.

How is it possible that in several countries in the world, there is not enough food, no work, no schools, no libraries, no proper sports facilities, no theatres, no adequate medical treatment or medicines when, within their boundaries can be found the most sophisticated arsenals of firearms, even very expensive items such as fighter planes? This is because governments in rich and developed countries are allowed, encouraged in fact, to assist those countries in the promotion of wars, so they must take the necessary steps to prevent those countries from becoming wealthy, modern countries The more the people feel oppressed and miserable, the more likely they are to revolt. The more people are divided, by religions, ethnicity, wealth, politics and nationality, the easier for the elite that runs the world to literally 'get away with murder'.

Of course there are NGO's that try to alleviate suffering and improve society generally, but, when for every airplane or lorry full of clothes, food, medicines, and practical aid, you have ten loaded with rifles and grenades, not much can be achieved.

This brings me to the subject of psychology and education. We live in a world where despite its permissiveness, if a film shows a couple in love having sex in an unusual way or position, censorship declares it pornographic and prohibits its viewing. There are a few European and American countries where explicit sex is allowed, but only to viewers above a certain age. However, films showing every kind of non-stop violence and atrocity, with blood flowing like waterfalls, are not only uncensored but also encouraged. Killing by hand, bullets or bombs is considered acceptable entertainment for people of any age. Violent characters often become heroes by the end of a film. The more they torture or kill people, the more they are admired, revered, respected or loved. So, how can we dream of a peaceful world, if we educate our citizens to believe that violence as opposed to love - will bring them power, respect and happiness. The promotion, through education, of human love, of understanding and compassion, should be a fundamental part of the activities and aims of all Human Rights organizations.

Human beings should have the RIGHT to an education that makes them humane, noble citizens who all respect human life. However, this education should be 100% lay and neutral. Theistic religions, ethnicity and patriotism are the seeds from which wars grow.

We should all have the right to an education that explains to us how we have lived up to now, why we have had two world wars, how they could have been avoided and what to do, if we wish to prevent World War III from becoming a reality in an era where greed, love of power, envy and lack of respect for human life pervades our world. With the third millennium, we must enlighten to the fact that we cannot be called human beings if we do not respect the life of other human beings regardless of colour, religion, race or ideology. Prejudice is based in ignorance and is frequently encouraged by politicians and the media, who stir up dissent by the very language used.

This brings me to my final point: Peace Journalism. We know that talking or writing about militias, terrorism, mortars, submarines, lucrative arms contracts, profits from war -even war memorials - has not brought, and will never bring about PEACE. But what is the PEACE-JOURNALISM OPTION? In its present form, it is mainly the promotion of fair, unprejudiced reporting with the inclusion of human-interest stories. The 'alternative media' gatherings I have attended were interesting. However, getting every journalist involved in a collective campaign to support the Olympics is not the same as bringing them all to a campaign supporting world Peace.

The American academic Neil Portman, says that journalists should not concern themselves with information and knowledge, but wisdom. The problem is: how can we make sure that a journalist has attained wisdom before he/she can transmit that wisdom to the world?

The parliamentary commission is wise in considering that political correspondents should register their outside interests in the same way as MPs but we all know from experience that this is not enough. Many MPs have failed to register their 'real' income, their outside interests, or at least their most crucial ones.

What we need is for prospective journalists to pass a 'wisdom test'. That test will show how universal and neutral their knowledge is! How can we bring peace about if there are still so many journalists who can't make a distinction between nationality and religion? How many times do we read things like: 'Polish, Germans and Jews'. Only when the day comes and we read: 'Christian and Jewish Poles, Christian and Jewish Germans', and so on, can we start to see the light of peace

Not long ago (this is from a letter I wrote in 1996 after a suicide bomb attack in a Tel Aviv café) two intelligent and educated journalists from Syria, one Muslim and one Christian, explained to me how Hitler had been sent by God, and how the young men who walk into cafés in Tel Aviv with bombs in their pockets are also sent by God. They both spoke of how the world is over-populated and how these 'envoys of God' help redress the balance. When I asked them why they did not plant bombs in the centre of Damascus or in the building where they lived, they were shocked at first. But as intelligent and sensitive people, they understood my message perfectly well. I then asked them if the young man who had exploded the bomb in Tel Aviv had done so in a café full of Moslems, would they have been celebrating the event.

This helped the journalists see how prejudiced they were. Prejudice will not disappear until governments and churches change the education they impart. They must teach all people that everybody's life is worthy of the same respect as their own, that all human beings have the right to live and that ALL people are EQUAL. I am always amused when a Pope preaches respect for all religions, yet, so easily forgets the century long Catholic campaigns to annihilate Protestants, Jews and Muslims. He also conveniently forgets how the entire Latin American Continent became Catholic through the invaders' orders, 'Convert or die'.

If the Pope is sincere when he continues to say that all religions are equally valid now that there is ample proof Jesus' mother was not artificially inseminated by God, and we know that naked children with wings do not exist, why does he not propose that all Catholics become Protestant? This could not happen. The Pope is paid to fight for his church. So, although he does preach unification, it is only if all Protestants become Catholics.

We also have the Moslem Brotherhood, who campaign for an all-Muslim world. Theistic religions will destroy the world. This may sound like a digression from Peace Journalism, but I cannot tire of stressing my firm belief that Gods, religions and Peace do not go together. Look at the Vatican citadel. Look at the Muslim citadels in Egypt and elsewhere. You can tell that these powerful religious corporations had only one thing in mind – or rather, three things: invade, kill, and conquer.

Peace Journalists should lobby all religious denominations in the pursuit of peace. Peace Journalists should expose the lust for power of the churches, the direct connection between churches and the worst atrocities in human history. It is not enough for the Pope to give apologies to the world for the Crusades or the Inquisition. He must apologize for the Vatican's involvement in two world wars and much more. The Pope should be made to explain why his 'rulings' results in so many more millions of unhappy people in the world. He should explain why he did not change his views after visiting Nigeria and witnessing so much poverty, misery, and millions living in the streets with not enough buses, not enough schools, not enough medical care and with thousands of children dying premature deaths because of lack of food. Did the Pope tell them the Catholic Church does not allow contraceptives? And what about the Aids epidemic? Does the Pope not care? Peace Journalists should act and write on these vital issues.

With the seven new mortal sins revealed by the Vatican, I have visions of the Pope and the entire Vatican going to confession on a daily basis! Every new sin - except for the seventh - is practiced by the occupants of this fortress and most of them are practiced by priests the world over. I list them:

Sin 1 - Drug Abuse: the amount of alcohol consumed at the Vatican reaches proportions that transform drink into drugs.

Sin 2 - Accumulating Excessive Wealth: this, from the richest organisation in the world.

Sin 3 - Causing Poverty: by not allowing the use of contraceptives, causing poverty is exactly what the Church does. This sin is doubled by the church accepting donations from the poor and trebled, by cynically encouraging poverty with its slogan, 'Jesus loves the poor'

Sin 4 - Social Injustice: without even considering the 'rich and poor' division they cause in the world, just think of the Palaces in which Bishops and Cardinals live and the living standards of the majority of human beings. Or, look at the different lifestyles between priests to the rich and priests to the poor.

Sin 5 - Environmental Pollution: every time the Pope wants to travel, he causes the same pollution as about 300 people, thanks to his regal sized retinue.

Sin 6 - Morally Debatable Experiments, Such As Cloning. This sin is very revealing. They mention 'cloning'. However, experiments of new weapons, new bombs, new torture techniques, these seem to be un-necessary to mention.

My impression is that if the Pope and his acolytes do not 'confess', they will all be condemned to hell. Something else for Peace journalists to write about!

If Peace journalists concentrated on people of different religions, ethnicity and nationalities, how they share a concert, a meal, a trip somewhere, this would be an educational starting point for the population of the world, who would follow their example. When the population of the world gets the message that all denominations can live happily together they will refuse war. When the message from the people to governments is, 'We all love each other. We respect the life of all people. We will not go to war', governments will have to close all weapon factories.

Politicians or church people who say anything that may incite revolt or aggression should be immediately exposed. Peace Journalists should expose arm manufacturers and dealers, both legal and illegal, their financial gains and losses, their relationship with politicians, religious groups and terrorist organizations. They should interview terrorists and mercenaries, analyse, and expose what made them what they are.

It is very interesting for the world to know the minds of terrorists and those behind them. For instance, some young Palestinian Muslims, who have even had Jewish girl friends, could not care less about religion or politics. They put a bomb in their pocket and walk to their death in a Tel Aviv café simply to show to their friends how virile they are, because they are promised that, if they kill Jews, God will reward them in heaven with a large number of young and beautiful virgins. They do not realise there is no sex-life in the after-life! Peace Journalists could also tell the world how these poor, innocent victims have been mentally and emotionally brainwashed and sometimes drugged before being taken to the chosen site.

Peace journalists should tell the world the similarities between Jews and Muslims - the tradition of circumcision, the prohibition of eating pork - stressing the fact that they all are descendants of Sem. In other words, they are all Semites. So killing each other is like killing your own brothers or cousin, as I said before.

Peace journalists should expose all the horrors of religious divisions through the wars these divisions have created, but also through the personal tragedies they create. I knew four Catholics, five Protestants, seven Moslems and four Jews who have all committed suicide because their parents opposed their marriage to a person from a different religious denomination.

Peace journalists should tell of the many beautiful love stories between enlightened people of different religious faiths. They would do a great job if, after studying the music of some ancient cultures like those of Tibet and Bolivia/Peru, they explained to the world how obvious it is that in the beginning, there was just one group of people, that divisions or separations appeared through natural modifications of our planet. The psychological considerations that every religion brought about should also be the subject of enlightened Peace journalism.

Peace journalists should also be able to describe the physical differences between human beings - people from Japan,

China, Ecuador, black, white and yellow skins and the gamut of skin colours in between - comparing not only the music, but also, other similarities between two very distant, geographically speaking, races, proving how originally these very different cultures and colours were one. This would be of paramount importance in our quest for human unification and Peace.

Love affairs of Popes, Cardinals and Bishops could be exposed, not as an invasion of privacy, but to show how we are all human beings with the same emotions and needs. Through this concentration on similarities rather than differences, through love rather than war, Bob Geldof, Madonna et al could call on the G8 Summits to abolish the Arms Trade, including all weapon research, campaigning then to rid the world of all financial institutions, whose success depends on brokering loans for military contracts. The scientists of the world could then be free to develop products that will prolong peoples' lives rather than brutally shortening them.

All steps on the Path to Peace.

Dear Ahed,

I have been thinking.

It is all very well that charities ask the City - I mean Banks- and industry to give more money, but it would seem they are not at all interested to know how the money they receive was made in the first place. Such a high percentage of donor companies make their colossal fortunes thanks to the wars and weapon deals they finance. In fact, once a war is over, a good percentage of donated money goes to help victims of war who lost their job, home, limbs, or family, who are displaced or refugees,

Would not it be better for humanity and for our planet, if the big donors and financiers stopped forever their assistance to warmongers and used just a fraction of that money to entertain politicians so that they have no time to think about invading countries, destroying them, starving or killing millions?

What about Banks practicing charity on politicians with one condition - that the country of whatever politician stops developing, manufacturing, selling or buying weapons. That all weapon factories are closed. No more air-fighters, no more warships, no more Armed Forces.

Governments would then have not billions but trillions for their National Health Services, medical research and education. Across the world there will be no more divide between industrial, wealthy, countries and a struggling Third World. There would be enough resources to feed the hungry until they are wealthy enough to feed themselves. Healthcare and education would then be available to everyone in the world. What a wonderful world we could have……

Oh, Ahed, what a wonderful world we could have!

Must go.

Alberto

ABOUT THE AUTHOR

Born in La Plata, Argentina, to parents of Russian and Romanian descent, Alberto Portugheis is an international pianist and teacher. After winning First Prize at the Geneva Concours de Virtuosité, Portugheis embarked upon an international career, visiting almost 50 countries. Aberto Portugheis performs as soloist with many major orchestras across the world. He frequently broadcasts on radio and television and gives regular Master-Classes. His acclaimed recordings include masterpieces from a repertoire of music ranging from baroque to contemporary.

In parallel with his career on the concert platform he works for peace. His vision is to achieve a just and peaceful world, free of war. He works to inspire people to respect human life, which he sees as the first requisite for achieving Human Rights, Justice and Peace. He is in regular contact with people from many troubled areas - Palestine, Israel, Nepal, Sri Lanka, Burma, Iraq, several African and Latin American countries.

Alberto Portugheis is founder member and Vice-chairman of the Beethoven Piano Society of Europe, Vice-chairman of the International Society for the Study of Tension in Performance, Vice-president of the European Piano Teachers' Association, Chairman of the Iberian and Latin American Music Society and founder of the Asociacion Latino-Americana de Pianistas Pedagogos. Many of his peace ideas developed from his career in music.

Nobel's message was that a reduction in weapons would, in addition to helping the Peace cause, resolve a major source of pollution and depletion of the earth's resources. Alberto Portugheis goes further, campaigning for abolition of weapons. His work is first and foremost about a 'united' humanity, where death only occurs through age, ill health, accident or a natural phenomenon.

Daisaku Ikeda, the great Peace campaigner and President of the Buddhist Society, Soka Gakkai International, is an inspiration to Alberto Portugheis, who is also a Buddhist. He supports the work and ideas for Conflict Solution of the founder of Transcend, Johan Galtung, but goes a step further, stressing, *'No matter how much we educate people to dialogue, by also providing them with weapons, this education becomes invalid.'* He supports all campaigns against nuclear arms, but is aware that the sophisticated conventional weaponry of today is almost as lethal. Portugheis also supports the Campaign Against Arms Trade (CAAT) but stresses that weapons are not made by Charities, but by companies that need to sell and trade them. He admires greatly and supports the work of his musician colleague, Daniel Barenboim, but from his personal experience of four decades of encouragement for Muslim and Jewish musicians to work together, it is clear that the results of these collaborations are far from the achievement of Peace.

The message of Alberto Portugheis is not comfortable. It requires a total change of perspective. Kant wrote '**Dare to know. That is the motto of Enlightenment**'. It is daring to know that has put Alberto Portugheis' life at risk - uncomfortable knowledge is the fuel with which he campaigns to educate and to promote a world without war.

Alberto Portugheis was nominated for the 2008 Nobel Peace Prize.